FRED MOORE'S KETTERING

By the same author:
Kettering Revisited: Pictures from the Past (1993 – reprinted 1999),
The Kettering Album: More Pictures from the Past (1997),
20th Century Kettering: A Book for the Millennium (1999)

Fred Moore's KETTERING

Tony Smith

W. D. WHARTON
WELLINGBOROUGH

This book is dedicated to the memory of
the late Fred Moore (1915–1999)
whose lifelong contribution to preserving
Kettering's history is reflected within its pages.

First published in 2003 by
W. D. Wharton
37 Sheep Street
Wellingborough
Northamptonshire NN8 1BX

Text copyright © Tony Smith 2003

Tony Smith asserts his moral right
to be identified as the author of this work

ISBN 1-899597-16-6

Designed and typeset by John Hardaker
Wollaston, Northants
Printed and bound in Great Britain by
Butler & Tanner Ltd
Frome, Somerset

END-PAPER CAPTIONS

Front (left)   Kettering Market Place and Parish Church
circa 1916.

Front (right)   Fred Moore in his shop in June 1991.

Rear (left)   Montagu Street, Kettering circa 1916.

Rear (right)   Dalkeith Place, Kettering circa 1916.

Contents

Acknowledgements

The photographs and postcards in this book are based on The Fred Moore Collection, except where stated, with additional pictures and advertising material from the author's own archives. Many of the images were originally published in the former *Kettering Leader* and the Northamptonshire *Evening Telegraph*, whose photographer Alan Castle took the pictures of Fred Moore on this page and the front end-paper. Thanks also go to David Capps of East Carlton for the use of his pictures of the Market Place, the Regal Cinema and VE Day celebrations, and Ralph Wood for his help with the Midland Band Club information. My usual enormous gratitude goes to the helpful staff at Kettering Reference Library, *Evening Telegraph* librarian Liz McBride, the book's designer John Hardaker of Wollaston and publisher Robert Wharton of W. D. Wharton, Wellingborough, who continues to support my work and grants me full editorial freedom for its content.

Most of all, the author will be forever indebted to Fred Moore's nephew, Alf Althorpe of Kettering, for the generous loan of his late uncle's unique and priceless historical legacy and for writing the foreword.

Bibliography

Kettering Leader (and *Guardian*) and *Kettering Observer*
Northamptonshire Evening Telegraph
The Fred Moore Collection
The Frank Thompson Collection
Old Kettering and its Defenders (1984) by Tony Ireson
Old Kettering – A View from the 1930s, Volumes 1 to 6 (1988–1999)
    by Tony Ireson
Kettering: Temp George V (1912)
F. W. Bull's *History of Kettering* (1891)
A History of Kettering Parish Church (1977) by Kettering Civic Society
A Walk Around Kettering (1972); *Lost and Hidden Kettering* (1974)
    by Kettering Civic Society
A Pictorial History of Kettering (1985) by The Rotary Club of Kettering Huxloe
Kettering: British Industries (1891) by the British Industrial Publishing Company
The Diamond Jubilee History of the Kettering Industrial Co-operative Society (1926)
Growth and Goodwill: The New Way by the Kettering Clothing Manufacturing
    Co-operative Society (1928)
*Torchbearers in History 1893-1943: Half a Century of Co-operative Industrial
    Fellowship* (1946) by Harold Taylor
The Rise of Industrial Kettering (1975) by R. L. Greenall
My Father (1936) by W. H. F. Timpson
Seventy Years Agrowing: An Early History of Timpsons (1938) by W. H. F. Timpson
A Century of Service: William Timpson Ltd 1865–1965 (1965) by D. J. Timpson
Mobbs Miller 1885–1985 (1985) by John Sexton
Kettering Gas Company 1834–1948 (1948) by T. N. Bird
Let's Go to the Pictures: 100 Years of Cinemas in Kettering (2000)
    by Maurice Thornton
Kettering and District General Hospital 1897-1997 (1997) by John Pettman
Cytringanian Farewell: Kettering Grammar/Boys School 1577–1993 (1995)
    by The Old Cytringanians
The School in the Horsemarket (1951) by John Lilley
Fuller Church, Kettering 1696–1946 by Gladys M Barrett
The Early History of St Andrew's Church, Kettering (1988)
Souvenir of the Opening of Kettering Free Library (1904)
Souvenir of the Coronation Festivities at Kettering (1902)
Official Programme of the Coronation Celebrations in Kettering (1911)
Official Programme of the Victory Celebrations in Kettering (1946)
A Wanderer in Northamptonshire (1948) by George Harrison
Kettering Town Football Club Handbook (1957-1958)
Whellan's *Directory of Kettering* (1884)
C. N. Wright's *Directory of Kettering* (1884)
Kettering Street and Classified Trades Directory (various)
Kelly's Directory of Northamptonshire (various)
Northamptonshire Past and Present (various)

This picture, also from the 1880s, shows a procession along Newland Street from the Gold Street corner to mark St Crispin's Day. St Crispin was the patron saint of shoemakers and an annual parade was held on October 25. The large house on the right was the home of John Wallis, who ran the flour mills at Burton Latimer with his brother. Mr Wallis was chairman of the Local Board for many years and married Mary Stockburn, sister of corset maker John Turner Stockburn. The bay-windowed house was for many years the home of shoe manufacturer George Cleaver, whose factory was in Lower Street, and later became the Mikado Cafe. The premises to its left were occupied by the shoe firm of Abbot & Bird. Bottom left of the picture is the corner shop of grocer and tea dealer Edwin Charles Garnsey.

This aerial view from the parish church was taken circa 1886 by Alfred Knighton of High Street, then the only photographer in Kettering. In the foreground is the Rectory, with the marks of a tennis court on the lawn clearly visible. The long, low building to its left in Church Walk is Wilmot's corset factory (later a steam laundry), which stands opposite the rear of the old police station before it was enlarged. Beyond in Market Street is the infant department of the Boys National School (later the weights and measures office), which faces the Parish Church School in Horsemarket. At the top of Market Street is the town's first fire station, later moved further down the street. On the corner of Carrington Street is the double-fronted house of Christopher Park on the site of the Liberal Club (erected in 1889). Of great interest to Poppies fans is the only known view (top right) of George Eldred's field (now the York Road and Tennyson Road area), the club's first home. Here crafty crowds would often stand looking over the hedge to get a free glimpse of home matches. The field was also used for rugby matches.

Another aerial view taken from the parish church from the opposite direction, overlooking Station Road and Headlands, which in those days ended at Hawthorn Road. In the foreground is what are now the Manor House gardens, then a big field with a huge tree in the middle, bounded by a buttressed grey wall which stretched from Sheep Street up Bowling Green Road to the cattle market gates. In the summer the field was filled once or twice with up to 3,000 hungry and excited Sunday School children on their annual treat. It was also often used as a meeting point before church parades or to celebrate Coronations and Jubilees. Bottom right in the picture are the Royal Iron Works of agricultural engineer William Smith, replaced in 1904 by the new library. The roadway by the foundry was very narrow, with no pavement on that side of Sheep Street until you got to the parish church fence. When this picture was taken, market gardens were on the other side of Bowling Green Road. Allotments can also be seen on the Sheep Street corner opposite Sawyer's Almshouses.

This High Street view from the 1890s shows the original Old White Horse Inn, with its distinctive pavement sign. To its right are premises used by boot and shoe maker Edward Smith and watchmaker Henry Scrivener. Mr Smith was the father of A. E. Smith, whose motor body building firm was established in Carrington Street in 1898 and survives today. Mr Scrivener was said to be the first Kettering tradesman to produce his own electric light. Just in view next door is the butcher's shop run by the London Central Meat Company on the corner of Huxloe Place. The landlord of the Old White Horse when this was taken was Jimmy Shortland, who brewed his own beer at the back, assisted by Sam Reed of the Robin Hood. The hotel was demolished in 1905 and rebuilt on the site of the aforementioned shops.

This Victorian view shows the shop of watchmaker and silversmith John Henry Wheeler at 5-7 High Street to the left of what is now the HSBC Bank. The premises, built on the site of a 17th century Weldon stone farmhouse, remain a jeweller's today after Thornton's moved there in 1969. Mr Wheeler built up a thriving business, taking on his nephew George Field as an apprentice and later as partner. Mr Field took over the business when Mr Wheeler died in 1887 and kept it going until his own death in the mid-1920s. It later became a wool shop for many years. The building next door was built by the Leicestershire Banking Company in the 1870s and was the Midland Bank for much of the last century until becoming HSBC.

This photograph was taken from Market Place, looking towards the High Street, in the late 1890s. At the foot of Market Street are the printing and publishing premises of Walter & John Goss, with part of the Northamptonshire Bank to their right. After serving an apprenticeship in his native town of Woburn, John went into business with his brother (previously living in Lancashire) in 1880. At first they worked from various departments in the town before taking over the former antiques shop run by Charles Pollard, with John running the stationery side of the business and Walter overseeing the printing and bookbinding. John was a warden at the parish church and founder member of the intriguingly titled Kettering & District Mutual Plate Glass Insurance Society. Walter was vice-president and treasurer of the Church Institute and a leading Conservative in the town. Both were firm Felons and Freemasons – John becoming Grand Master. In 1898 the corner property was bought for £2,070 by the council for road widening, so they moved along the High Street to the site where Woolworths now stands. A striking new corner entrance was erected at the turn of the century for the bank, which was later re-named the Capital & Counties and later Lloyds. The corner was turned into Yo-Yo's noodle bar this year. The Goss brothers died within six months of each other – John in December 1916, aged 59, and Walter in June, 1917, aged 60.

The origin of Bakehouse Hill – the former triangular island at the junction of Gold Street and High Street – goes back centuries, its name deriving from a common bakehouse which stood there during the reign of Elizabeth I. Leased by the Crown, it was known as the King's bakehouse in Charles I's time and is clearly shown on Thomas Eyre's map of Kettering in 1720. It was demolished in 1865 and replaced by Joseph Allen's bakery, pictured left, and remained in the Allen family until Theobald's took it over in 1936. It kept the Theobald name after being bought out by Adams of Northampton in 1960 but was pulled down in Phase One of the town centre redevelopment of Gold Street.

Bakehouses

Another public bakehouse used by generations of Kettering people stood on a central site at the top of Huxloe Place. When this picture (right) was taken in the 1890s, it was still run as a bakery by Joseph Meadows, who also owned premises in Stamford Road. The building came down in April 1923 to provide room for extensions to the printing works of the *Evening Telegraph* and *Kettering Leader*. The new works and editorial offices were then among the largest in the Midlands. Another ancient building to go was Chater's farmhouse, occupied in its final 30 years by George Mason, who ran a general store in Mill Road.

This wonderful close-up of the old Post Office and Arcade in Gold Street, taken just before the turn of the last century, is probably the earliest surviving photograph of the terracotta block. The impressive buildings, designed by Gotch & Saunders, were erected in 1887 and comprised the Post Office and seven new shops. Behind the Royal Hotel handcart in the picture is the famous arcade which led through to Tanners Lane, Richard Leys and Northall Street. On its right is the drapery on Frank Jesse Vine. Kettering's first post office, under postmistress Sarah Stockburn, was established around 1800 next to the Cherry Tree pub in George Street. Her successor Miss Elizabeth Tibbs moved it next door to the Toller Church in Gold Street in 1854 and, until the railway arrived three years later, mail still arrived by stagecoach or cart. When Miss Tibbs married milliner Sam Woolston in 1859, his former High Street shop opposite the New White Horse Hotel became the post office and he was appointed postmaster. For the next 31 years the couple worked together, the last two as the first occupants of the new Gold Street office. Mrs Woolston retired six months after her husband died in 1890, having held the record of being – at 70 – the oldest postmistress in the service. When she left, there were five town postmen and six covering surrounding villages.

The extremely rare picture on the left was taken around 1880 and shows the original Robin Hood pub at the bottom of Northall Street, complete with thatched roof. The building went back to the mid-18th century, but the exact date is not known, although in days of yore it was the venue for many exciting cock fights. Travelling showmen with their dancing bears (see page 78) also lodged there. Pictured on the right are old houses opposite the Robin Hood in 1870. The old farmhouse with its thatched roof, just in view, stood on the corner of Field Street.

This astonishing picture is the only known photograph of the first Kettering-owned motor car in motion. The vintage vehicle, seen here in a blur having just entered the top of Gold Street from the crossroads, was an 1898 Benz Comfortable. The two-seater, single-cylinder model belonged to William Hunt, known as Peter, whose family had a coachbuilding business making horse-drawn vehicles at a workshop in Montagu Street, where Kettering Health Foods now stands. One of Mr Hunt's workers collected the 3hp motor from London, averaging 12mph on the trip back to Kettering. Mr Hunt sold it on to a Brigstock farmer and in 1933 the car was found rusting on an allotment, where it had been dumped by Regent Street scrap dealer William Clarke, who acquired it at a farm sale. It was then bought for £4 by Veteran Car Club member Mr H. K. Jacques of Orlingbury Hall, who planned to restore it to enter the London to Brighton car rally, but its whereabouts were lost during World War Two.

The ornate archway pictured at the top of Gold Street was erected for the Northants Agricultural Show held in Kettering on 14 and 15 June 1898. The motto on the other side of the arch read "May Local Industries Flourish". Flags fluttered from every shop and Venetian masts bearing streamers were also erected every 35 yards from Station Road to the Buccleuch Hotel (then the edge of town). The show site was in a field off Stamford Road, opposite Grange Farm. The first day was attended by a record 900 people, each paying half a crown admission. Some 3,000 ft of shedding, stands and paddocks were built for exhibits, plus stalls for horses and cattle, with tents for sheep. These surrounded a main arena, complete with bandstand. The three-storey Georgian house beyond the archway in the photograph, standing on the Montagu Street – Silver Street corner, belonged to veterinary surgeon Trevor Spencer.

Welcome to the first of four fascinating pages illustrating the major restoration work at Kettering Parish Church from April 1890 to September 1892. The mammoth project cost a total of £9,000 which was £2,000 more than estimated, and came about after the then Duke of Buccleuch said in passing to the rector, Canon Henry Lindsay (referring to the pews), "When are you going to clear out the old sheep pens from the church?" A public fund was started, a plan of action was prepared by the notable architect Sir Arthur Blomfield, and Messrs Margetts & Neal were the contractors. The work amounted to a complete overhaul of the 13th century church, as witnessed in these historic pictures. The pews were indeed removed, but some of the old oak woodwork was bought by Dr Roughton to use as panels in his Northampton Road home (later the site of the bus station). During restoration Sunday services were held at the nearby Corn Exchange.

During restoration, the roof was stripped and the lead taken off, but the condition of the timber there was much worse than expected. This picture was taken by keen amateur photographer Ernest Bishop, who was church organist and choirmaster for almost 50 years. The eight workmen were employed by John Cooper, who had the plumbing contract, and were responsible for laying 40 tons of lead on the roof. Pictured from left are Mr H. E. Cooper, son of the contractor, Mr E. Winsor, James Stanley, John Cooper, Mr J. Flowers and the Loveday brothers from Northampton. Far right is Mr W. Clipston of Geddington. Amazingly, some local couples were married in the chancel of the sacred edifice during the period when the roof of the nave was off and the flooring had been taken up!

The main picture shows how much the parish church was gutted during the restoration. At night, with braziers on the floor, the scene must have been unforgettable. The smaller photograph shows John Cooper taking down the western clock dial to be repaired by Leesons of Birmingham. William Horden had charge of the clock machinery and the builder was Charles Andrews. When the spire was restored, the mistake was made of fastening the stonework by iron bands. These rusted and expanded the stone so much that further work was necessary later on.

This historic scene shows the parish church bells outside the west door about to be re-hung. Standing behind the two bells on the right is Canon Lindsay, who was rector of Kettering from 1853 to 1892. Seven of the eight bells previously recast and increased in number in 1714 were removed on 8 August, 1890 to be re-tuned and renovated by J. Taylor & Co. at Loughborough. The old No. 3 bell, which had never been in tune with its fellows, was replaced by a new one, paid for by local builder and keen campanologist Henry Henson. The church officially re-opened with a special service on 21 September, 1892 (St Matthews's Day), conducted by the Bishop of Peterborough, Dr Creighton. Sadly, Canon Lindsay, who instigated the work, died in April that year. In 2002 a Jubilee Appeal was launched to raise £120,000 to replace all 12 bells with a new ring of 13.

Old photographs of Kettering don't come much rarer than this classic scene of a horse and cart cantering over the Gold Street crossroads into Montagu Street in 1897. The premises at the top of Gold Street (previously occupied by grocer Edwin Garnsey – see page 11) belonged to clothier, jeweller and pawnbroker W. H. Baker. He came to Kettering from his native Hull just a year before this picture was taken and became very involved in town affairs, serving on the urban council and numerous committees. A closer view of the picturesque building to the right of Baker's along Newland Street can be seen on page 14 of my first book, *Kettering Revisited*, when it was Lottie Bryant's fruit and vegetable shop. When this photograph was taken, the business was run by Mrs W. Tansley.

"The Pav"

The Gaumont Pavilion, which stood to the right of the New White Horse in High Street, is fondly remembered by all as "The Pav". Initially it was called the Kettering Electric Pavilion and when it opened on 10 May 1913, the only other 'picture houses' in the town were Vint's Palace on the Market Place, the Avenue in Russell Street and the Victoria Hall in Gold Street. The "Pav" was taken over by Gaumont in 1927 and received a facelift in the 1950s, when this picture was taken. When it closed in October 1959, the building was pulled down and replaced by the new Boots store. The Pavilion scored a hat-trick of 'firsts' for Kettering – its first purpose-built cinema, the first to show 'talkies' and the first to run continuous performances. It was also one of the pioneers of the new 'wide-screen'.

This picture (left) was taken before the Electric Pavilion was built, when it was the home of John Newman, a tanner and leather merchant with premises in High Street and Lower Street. The buildings to the right of Newman's were occupied by the hairdresser, tobacconist and milliner Henry Field and (just in view) grocer Edward Hale. Much later Field's premises became the town's branch of the Leicester Building Society (now Alliance & Leicester) and Hale's became Civil's supermarket until 1980 (now Dixons).

You can never have too many pictures of the old Kettering Grammar School building in Gold Street, which was shamefully demolished by the council (without notice or consultation) one quiet Sunday morning in November 1964. This wonderful view from 1905 shows some pupils outside (presumably with their mothers). This was the school's home from 1856 until 1913 when it moved to new premises in Bowling Green Road, later shared with the High School and now, of course, the council offices. The Gold Street building later became the home and surgery of Dr Daniel Drake-Lee until the early 1930s when a new surgery was built in Lower Street. The doctor then went to live at a house in Rockingham Road, which became SATRA House, headquarters of the town's shoe research association.

This fascinating scene was captured on camera outside what is now the HSBC bank in High Street. It shows the chaos caused by Kettering Urban Council's steam-roller when it broke down on Monday, 17 May 1909. Nicknamed 'Tommy Dodd' the elephantine vehicle remained there for most of the day while its large rolling reels, gear wheels, axles and other machinery were dismantled and repaired. It attracted much attention from passing shoppers but a beat bobby (remember them?) was there to keep an eye on things. A story also appeared in the *Kettering Leader* beneath the headline "T. D. Indisposed: Open Air Treatment in Kettering High Street"!

This historic wartime photograph was taken on Tuesday 31 August 1943, when a detachment of 150 coloured American troops marched down Gold Street en route to a "swing drill" on the Market Place. Standing in as temporary sergeant was 12-year-old Patrick Wright of Rockingham Road, who marched alongside them from Fuller Baptist Church where the parade began. Taking over from Major Curtis Miller, the young boy wore the same uniform worn by his father at the age of 14 during the previous war. The *Kettering Leader* reported that this purely improvised drill was used solely by coloured servicemen "who, with their perfect sense of rhythm, are adept at this kind of showmanship". The most impressive part of the parade was the accompanying chant and snatches of marching songs. As shown in the picture, the spectacle was also filmed for Movietone News and subsequently screened at local cinemas. (*Tony Smith Collection*)

This picture (left) of Horsemarket in the 1950s features some interesting buildings. On the left is the gable end of the Parish Church School, built as the Boys National School in 1873 and demolished in 1970. In the distance, with the parish church as a backdrop, is the radio and electrical shop owned by radio pioneer Paul Taylor. He joined his father's bicycle business in Silver Street (see page 91), added the retailing of radios in 1922 and took over the shop on his father's death in 1932. In the centre of the picture are the old corn stores (where I bought ammunition for my pea-shooter as a boy!) and art specialists and picture-framers Dinsdale's (still trading). Frederick Lawrence Dinsdale, chairman of the town's arts society, founded the business in 1927 and the shop has been run by Tony and Mary Hardy since 1974. Right of the picture is the Woolpack Inn (now Henry's) but the original pub it replaced went back hundreds of years. In its glory years in the mid-18th century, it boasted stabling for 40 horses, pens for 200 sheep and two commons for cows.

This town centre picture (right) from September 1921 shows workmen digging up the old wooden blocks in the High Street for resurfacing. The blocks had been laid 12 years earlier and those that were still useable were re-laid in Gold Street. Local landmarks here are the Old White Horse Hotel on the right, Wells the grocers on the left and the Webb Brothers' central clothing store in the mid-distance. The business was founded in 1789 and, in its heyday, boasted branches in ten other towns, as well as a sister shop in Kettering's Market Street opened six years after this picture was taken.

Cyclists, handcarts and horse-drawn traps were still the main forms of transport when this postcard was published during the First World War. The picture was taken from the High Street looking towards Bakehouse Hill and Gold Street. The prominent outfitters shop at No. 38 on the right was run at this time by Miss Annie L. Jenkinson, who took over the business from her father William Stafford Jenkinson after he died in December 1915 aged 82. Mr Jenkinson, son of Edward Jenkinson, was described as a hosier and a well-known figure in the town. He was first apprenticed to Ed Crump, whose High Street premises were almost opposite the shop he was to establish in the 1890s. He was a Sunday School teacher and senior deacon at Fuller Baptist Church, singing in its choir for some 60 years. On Bakehouse Hill we can see Allen's bakehouse (see page 16) and Horden's jewellers (see page 89). (*Tony Smith Collection*)

The chapter closes with two more views of the old Post Office buildings taken from opposite ends of Gold Street. The one on this page was taken in 1908 and gives a rare close-up of the Victoria Hall, with a group of boys and a lady with her pram standing under the awning. The building, designed by Gotch & Saunders and built by Margetts & Neal in 1888, became the lifeblood of late Victorian entertainment in Kettering. In front of its archway entrance were two ornate gas lamps, their glass displaying the words 'Victoria Hall', and the removable seating, including balcony and gallery, could hold from 1,000 to 1,200 people. As well as stage plays, concerts and opera, the hall hosted public meetings, religious gatherings, bazaars, balls and animated picture shows. Photographer Warren East displayed his wondrous lantern slides there – the first in the town – and hugely popular variety acts were booked by Gold Street music shop owner Alf Bailey, whose company took over the hall in 1907. He also led a string orchestra which often accompanied shows from the stage pit. The hall was converted to a cinema, which opened on 23 August 1920 with the Mary Pickford film *Ragamuffin*. The final show as a theatre was a production by Basil Mitchell's London company of the play *The Lowland Wolf*, which ran in the week beginning 5 April that year. The business between the Victoria Hall and the Post Office belonged to grocer Henry John Bye, who moved to the town from his native Brampton in Oxfordshire in 1887. He became president of the Kettering & District Grocers' & Tea Dealers' Association and for many years judged at the annual Grocers' Exhibition at the Agricultural Hall. Mr Bye also served on the urban council's education committee.

The Proclamation of King George V took place on the Market Place on Wednesday 11 May 1910. The reading was given by the High Sheriff of Northamptonshire, in court dress, from a special platform for civic leaders and VIPs erected in front of Vint's Electric Palace. The guard of honour at the ceremony consisted of the Yeomanry, Territorials (under Lt Wilson), the fire brigade (under Captain Riddle), the ambulance division (under Chief Supt E. R. Lane) and police (under Sgt Hooper). Shops and factories closed and schoolchildren were given a half-day holiday to attend and flags were raised after being at half-mast when the king died. Public representatives gathered at the Royal Hotel, where the Sheriff was robed, and every vantage point was thronged, including the balconies of the cinema and the Geisha Tea Rooms next door (see picture). Even the top of the parish church nave was occupied and the more daring even climbed a high telephone pole. A short parade of public bodies marched across the road from the hotel for the Proclamation, which was followed by the National Anthem and a peal of bells. A vote of thanks was given by urban council chairman Cllr L. E. Bradley, met by much cheering, waving of handkerchiefs and a chorus of "Hip, hip, hooray!" Kettering was the only town outside Northampton where the High Sheriff personally performed the Proclamation. (*Tony Smith Collection*)

This wartime photograph shows members of the Scottish Horse Regiment being inspected on the Market Place before heading for France in April 1915. The men had been billeted in the town for six months, winning many friends, attending dances at the Victoria Hall and exercising their horses on the Boughton Estate. Before their departure with the expeditionary force for the Dardanelles, Trooper Douglas Macdonald wrote an article in the *Kettering Leader* thanking their hosts for making them so welcome and for the "tender ties" forged between local girls and the garrison. Waxing lyrical, he said: "It was inevitable from the first that some of the sturdy and hardy would capitulate to those dancing eyes that smiled ever so coyly on us as we marched through the streets. Some of us have surrendered completely to the bombardment of eyes and lips, and have joined in the dissoluble bands of matrimony. Others, more canny as befits our Scottish nature, have plighted our troths under the trees amid the romantic glamour of Wood Lane and left engagement rings to keep us in memory until a more peaceful day shall dawn." The regiment left in three trains from Kettering station, the last including 30 four-wheeled wagons for the horses. How many were reunited with their sweethearts we shall never know.

This moving Market Place scene was captured on the morning of Wednesday 10 May 1945, as thousands of Kettering people attended a united open-air thanksgiving service for VE Day. Many wore black in memory of a son or husband lost in the war, some thinking perhaps of a brother or friend still fighting in the Far East. All gathered with new hope in their hearts to give thanks for the deliverance of their country from the six-year nightmare of conflict. The ceremony was conducted by three Free Church ministers and one Church of England clergyman, with a stirring and uplifting address from the Mayor, Cllr G. B. Smith. All windows facing the Market Place were thrown open and, as well as those braving the pouring rain around the platform of dignitaries, hundreds more lined adjacent streets. The Reverend Gordon Clark, Rector of Barton Seagrave, said prayers, followed by the general thanksgiving, said by all. Toller Church minister, the Reverend E. Keith Doman, led the intercessory prayers, followed by prayers for pardon, renewal and dedication. Young and old joined in the hymns and the service closed with the last two verses of the National Anthem beginning "God bless our native land." The public holiday was even observed by the *Evening Telegraph*, which failed to publish that day although reporters and photographers were out and about covering street parties and other festivities for the next day's edition. (*David Capps Collection*)

These Market Place celebrations took place on the evening of Monday 10 September 1935, when crowds of more than 10,000 welcomed home the Munn & Felton Works Band two days after winning the National Brass Band Championships at Crystal Palace at the first attempt. Bandsmen paraded the town in a decorated bus, followed by jubilant fellow shoe workers waving flags. Speeches were made from a platform in front of a floodlit Corn Exchange after the victors were greeted by urban council chairman, Cllr Charles Mayes. Musical director Stan Boddington then conducted a spirited rendition of Death Or Glory, before the band's president Fred Felton thanked the public for their support. The band also played Abide With Me as a tribute to recently departed Cllr Thomas Seddon, bandmaster with Kettering Rifle Band from 1886 to 1903. The band, formed only two years earlier by Mr Felton, went on to win five more UK titles as well as the World Championship under its later name, the GUS (Footwear) Band. The picture was taken from an upper window of the Market Hill offices of Drury's the builders. (*David Capps Collection*).

This final picture, taken from the top corner of the Market Place in December 1961, again shows the popularity of the market even in mid-winter as shoppers wrap up against the cold (maybe you recognise some of them?). It seems sad that despite a £250,000 revamp a few years ago, the number of stallholders has drastically diminished. Ironically, when work was being carried out, traders reported better business when moved to a temporary site in the town centre.

4. The Co-op

The Co-op played an important and influential role in the growth and development of Kettering. The first co-operative in the town was formed way back in 1829, when the majority of its then population of just over 3,000 lived in one-storey thatched cottages and suffered pitiful wages. The society's bid to alleviate such poverty failed but when a new generation tried again in 1866, it was the start of a revolution in the fortunes of the working-class over the following century. The first shop run by the Kettering Industrial Co-operative Society was in the front room of a house in High Street, where Sketchley now stands. After a slow start funds allowed the purchase of what became known as the No. 1 store on the top corner of Bakehouse Hill in 1871. Over half a century later KICS boasted 13 grocery stores and 10 butcher's shops and many other departments, selling everything from bread, milk and coal to drapery and confectionery. Not only did the Co-op reformers establish large factories for the production of clothes and shoes, providing work for thousands of men and women, but the movement also built large housing estates for its employees to live in. Its crowning glory came in October 1929 with the opening of the Central Hall in Montagu Street, followed in May 1930 by the magnificent Central Stores – Kettering's first department store. The above pictures show the two entrances to the elegant Central Arcade – Newland Street on the right and Montagu Street on the left. These, and the other splendid pictures in this chapter, come from a home-made souvenir photo album marking this memorable milestone in Kettering's history.

We begin with two views of building work in progress on the huge project, this one (left) taken of the Central Hall site in January 1929. The construction work was carried out by the Co-op's own building department to designs by Mr R. J. Williams, the acclaimed architect responsible for the commanding Timpson's shoe factory in Bath Road earlier that decade. The woodwork, fixtures, fittings and the maple dance floor in the hall were also done by the Co-op's works department, and the oil-fired central heating system was provided by Messrs Horrocks & Sons of Kettering and Northampton. The main arcade entrance in Montagu Street was between the Lutona Chocolate Shop and the Co-op's hairdressing salon. It was dome-lit and built in red Peterhead granite, paved with mosaic tiles leading to marble steps at the hall entrance. The Co-op's previous hall was in Tanners Lane.

This view (right) shows men at work on the site of the Central Store in Newland Street in April 1930. Old stables and an ugly yard off St Andrew's Street at the rear were dispensed with. A lot of excavating was necessary to make the store's floor levels suit the arcade's slight slope upwards to Montagu Street and the floor of the Newland Street front had to be made. All the divisional walls on the ground floor were removed, the superstructure being held up with girders and stanchions. All the framing for the shop windows, showcases and sun-blinds was done in bronze. The former butcher's and grocery shops and the front of the gentlemen's outfitting shop were gutted to form the Newland Street entrance. Building work began early in January by more than 80 men, and to keep them up to scratch two notice boards were put up, one saying: "Rome was not built in a day, but this store opens on May 28, 1930" and the other "You said you could do it by May 28".

The new Central Hall was one of the most modern in the UK and boasted one of the finest dance floors in the Midlands. Described as a "hall of a hundred uses", it seated 850 (602 downstairs) and included a smoking lounge, dressing rooms and kitchens capable of catering for 600 people. The Long Room upstairs (formerly a hay loft) could seat 160 people for whist drives, tea parties and wedding receptions (my late parents hired it for theirs). The Junior Guild Room in Eden Street could seat another 900.

The elegant, partly oak-panelled hall measured 69 ft 6 in by 42 ft 6 in, with a main balcony and smaller minstrel or dance-band balcony. For almost 50 years the multi-purpose auditorium hosted thousands of stage shows, concerts, public and political meetings and sporting events, including boxing bouts and even the finals of the World Snooker Championship in 1934, when the legendary Joe Davis beat Tom Newman by 25 frames to 22. Downstairs seating could be removed for dinners and dances, whilst a revolving mirrored pendant was suspended from the vaulted Art-Deco ceiling, with its decorative glass panels. There was also a projection room for showing films and a grand piano for musical events was supplied by Palmer's Music Stores in Dalkeith Place. Scenery for plays could be unloaded in St Andrew's Street straight onto the stage. Parking and stabling was provided in a yard behind the Fleur de Lys pub. The opening ceremony was performed by KICS president Thomas Adams and in the evening there was a concert by the Kute Kic(k)s.

The formal opening of the Central Stores, including extensions to the existing drapery, men's outfitting and boot departments, was held on Saturday 31 May 1930. It was to have been performed by Minister of Health Arthur Greenwood, but after being hurt in a fall, his wife deputised at the last minute. Two other Government ministers attended the ceremony, causing Prime Minister Ramsey MacDonald to send an amusing message asking the KICS not to take all the members of his Cabinet away from their duties that day. The stores were described by the *Evening Telegraph* as a "remarkable feat of engineering" comparable with any department store in London. Much of the floor space was occupied by glass showcases and 'island' fixtures and tiled customer toilets were found on both the ground and first floors. Among many new features was a dust-proof tailor rack holding 120 men's suits, which could be swung out and turned around, and swing mirrors in the men's and ladies' oak fitting rooms. There were four shoe-fitting and show rooms, for ladies, children, men and boys respectively, and an 18 ft domed lamp hung over the oak staircase to the first and second floor. There was a tea-room for staff, who also had their own roof garden for relaxation during breaks. The *ET* reporter was fulsome in his praise, writing: "With the Central Hall and its wonderful Arcade, which are blended with it so harmoniously, it represents the crowning triumph of the society's long list of notable achievements. There is nothing to compare with it for many miles around. It has made shopping a scientific pleasure. The Arcade is already a popular rendezvous – who would walk in the streets when such a charming and luxurious alternative offers itself?"

Millinery section on the first floor.

Mantle department on the first floor.

Drapery section.

Outfitting section.

THIS TABLET
IS IN GRATEFUL REMEMBRANCE OF THE
FOUNDERS AND WORKERS
OF THE
KETTERING INDUSTRIAL
CO-OPERATIVE SOCIETY, LTD
(ESTABLISHED 1866)
WHO HAVE PASSED AWAY.
THEIR COURAGE, INTEGRITY AND SELF
SACRIFICING DEVOTION TO CO-OPERATION
HAS MADE POSSIBLE THE ERECTION OF
THIS CENTRAL HALL AND CENTRAL ARCADE.
1930.

The men involved in building the Central Hall and Arcade – all KICS employees under building manager George (Ted) Ballard – are pictured here along with a rear view of the hall in Eden Street and a memorial bronze plate which hung in the Arcade. The group photograph had pride of place in the lounge of the Central Hall, which was (scandalously, if you ask me) mothballed in the mid-1970s. It remained largely unused (except for storage) until the new century arrived and is now a nightclub and bistro.

5. Kettering at Work

Kettering will forever be associated with the manufacture of boots and shoes. This wonderful photograph, taken in Northall Street in 1890, shows one of the earliest footwear factories in the town and the oldest when the firm of Charles East Ltd went into receivership in 1964. Charles was one of 11 children, whose youngest brother, artist Sir Alfred East, was born within yards of the factory, known as the Britannia Works. This former commercial traveller went into the shoe trade in 1854, helped by sons Walter and Frederick, who succeeded him on his death in 1875 and were joined by Sir Alfred from 1876 to 1880. Frederick's son, another Charles, took over in 1903 and was managing director from 1948 to the firm's demise. His son (another Frederick) became the fourth generation of the family to become director in 1942. The business began in Lower Street, moved to the Northall Street factory in 1863 and was enlarged in 1869. The handsome block at the front was added in 1882, joined by the five-storey block to its right in 1890. The firm was the first in town to use closing machines (1859), to make boots with riveted soles (1862) and to install a steam engine to drive the machines (1869). It also introduced sole sewing machines (1876), the American-made revolution press (1887), and generated its own electricity for lighting ten years before the town had its own supply. The company supplied footwear throughout Britain and its colonies, even providing hand-sewn and watertight boots for a 40-man Commonwealth Antarctic expedition led by Dr Vivian E. Fuchs. Walker Last were the final occupants of the factory, which was demolished in 1984 to make way for the Windsor Gardens old peoples' complex.

The wonderful evocative photographs on this page and opposite tell their own story, giving a glimpse of life inside one of Kettering's busy boot and shoe factories early last century. They were taken inside Mobbs Bros' Northall Works in Northall Street circa 1908, showing the hand-made methods used at that time. As seen in the right hand picture on this page, young boys would often follow their fathers into the trade, running errands, brushing floors and making tea for others in their department. Established in 1882, the firm provided employment for generations of Kettering men and women, later naming the factory the Embekay Works after one of its brands of footwear. The company moved to Durban Road following a terrible fire in 1922, which destroyed much of the works and contents valued at £20,000. By that time Mobbs had an output of 4,000 pairs of shoes per week, employing more than 200 people. It later specialised in sportswear and eventually amalgamated with Frank Wright & Company, moving to the latter's Carey Street works in Kettering in the 1960s. The Durban Street factory was vacant for a while before being bought by Carrington Street leatherdressers Davies & Company.

Kettering shoe company Smith, Sheffield & Foster, established in Sackville Street in 1895, was a palace of industry founded by Edward Smith of Kettering, William Sheffield of Corby and J. W. Foster of Rothwell. Here men are pictured in the press and fitting-up room of the company's Premier Works, built in Morley Street in 1901 and expanded in 1908. The firm produced all kinds of gents' and youths' boots (as well as its own gas and electric light) and adopted the spire of Kettering Parish Church as its trademark. In the picture men are cutting the heavy leather into the parts for the foundations of the shoes. Specially tanned hides were cut into soles, insoles, stiffeners and top pieces for the heels. These were then sorted, graded, moulded and "fitted up" with uppers from the closing room.

A 'pulling over' team is pictured (right) at work preparing the shoe for the 'Rex' puller-over, an almost human machine which could judge tension, not only pulling the upper tightly over the last but fixing it instantly with seven tacks. Following the departure of Mr Sheffield, the company continued as Smith & Foster and by the First World War was inherited by their respective sons, Frank Smith and Ernest Foster, the former being a director of the Liberal Club. 'Spire' became the name of one of the firm's brands of shoe, others being Premier, Bestofal, Helm, Stirling and Favourite. During The Great War, the company made thousands of boots for the British army.

This superb picture shows the 800 employees at work in the large machine room of the Co-op's gents clothing factory in 1930. The society was severely tested during the First World War, when a heavy withdrawal of men took place, and during the post-war slump from 1918 to 1927. But in 1929 it embarked on a great expansion and reorganisations scheme in Kettering, which included a warehouse extension and the doubling of the size of the ladies factory. A new plant for 500 workers was built in Oakley Road, Corby in 1938 and before the Second World War the society employed a high proportion of women aged 19 to 25. The company also provided a large sports ground for its employees and a shed for 350 cycles – the main form of transport to work in those days.

Our last look at the Co-op clothing factory (until page 65) shows nurses at practice in the assembly room of its Cobden Street premises at that time. The works had its own nursing division with members holding First Aid and Home Nursing certificates. Apart from First Aid, the nurses were always ready to attend employees who were ill at home or needed special treatment, for which they were paid by the society. Their uniforms, of course, were also made in the factory. Largely influential was the remarkable Walter Dyson, head of the factory welfare services, who clocked up an amazing 64 years as a member of the town's St John Ambulance Brigade. Throughout his 40 years' service to Kaycee, he was also a member of the factory fire brigade and its chief for 29 years.

This interesting aerial view of Kettering gasworks was taken in 1924 by Surrey Flying Services of what was then called the London Terminal Aerodrome at Croydon. The Kettering Gas Company was formed after a meeting of 25 leading townsmen on 13 December 1833, only 18 years after the defeat of Napoleon at Waterloo and four years before Queen Victoria ascended to the throne. The first management committee was chaired by John Cooper Gotch and by the end of May 1834 a quarter acre of land at the lower end of what is now Meadow Road was purchased for the construction of the works. The Kettering Gas Light & Coke Company was formed on 18 August that year with a capital of £2,500 divided into 100 shares of £25 each. The first gas was made at the works on Friday 31 October, with the first public lighting of 40 lamps in the town that evening, celebrated by a public subscription dinner at the Peacock Inn the next day. The above photograph showing the two gasholders was taken before the building of Northfield Avenue. To help get your bearings, Northampton Road is top left, with the railway line cutting across the picture from left to right. The big building bottom left is Bryan & Son's shoe factory, which burned down in a spectacular fire in the 1930s. It was later rebuilt as Aquascutum and is now the staff car park of Morrisons. The chimney just visible bottom right is from Thomas Geary's leather works. Meadow Road (middle left) was originally named Goosepasture Lane, but became Gas Street for obvious reasons.

This photograph of the gasworks, probably taken in the late 1920s or early 1930s, shows a Garrett steam wagon used to carry coal around the gasworks site. Before Northfield Avenue was built, the coal was brought from the goods yard at Kettering railway station by a pair of traction engines, hauling their dirty wagons through the town to Gas Street via Sheep Street, Market Place and High Street. The large three-storey building with the chimney stack, on the right of the photograph and seen emitting smoke in the centre of the previous page, was the retort house. Built just before the First World War, this incorporated the coal store and was where the gas was made.

This striking picture shows men at work inside the retort house at the gasworks. This was installed in 1912 as part of a major reconstruction of the works to take full advantage of improvements in the technique of gas production. Coal was baked by a big coke furnace, giving up its gas and becoming white hot coke, which was then added to the furnace. The new retort house and store had a capacity of one million cubic feet per day. In the new plant the drawing and charging of the 64 horizontal retorts was carried out entirely by mechanical power instead of the old hand labour method. In 1922 a carburetted water gas plant was installed to supplement the existing coal-gas process and reduce dependence on coal supplies. After nationalisation of the gas industry in 1949, production of coal gas continued at Kettering. The arrival of natural gas from the North Sea in the 1960s had a dramatic effect on consumption and rid town landscapes everywhere of their ugly gas holders and retort houses. The Kettering works eventually closed down in 1966.

This chapter closes with two historic photographs of gas mains being put down in Kettering town centre more than 100 years ago. The pictures are part of a series taken by local photographer Charles Speight, whose studios stood for many years at the junction between London Road and Bowling Green Road (see page 93). The scene on the left was taken in Sheep Street on 11 October 1897 – just a week after the first paper rolled off the presses of the *Evening Telegraph*. Little has changed – in the background is the Cherry Tree Inn next to Ernest Woodcock's first drapery shop (now Linnett's newsagents). The building on the far left is now occupied by the Red Rose restaurant. The right-hand picture was taken in Newland Street on 9 March 1898, with the premises of corn dealer William Thomas West on the left and Phillips' drapery on the right. The latter only closed down in July 2002 after 113 years in the town. The pictures were saved by gas company worker Roy Goodfellow when the works were demolished.

6. Kettering at Play

Because of the First World War, Kettering's Co-op Clothing Society put back plans to celebrate its 21st anniversary originally scheduled for 1915. But it made amends on 10 October 1919 with a tremendous tea party for more than 1,000 workers and friends at its new factory in Field Street. Every employee received a 'coming of age' gift – a wallet for the men and a fancy needle case for the ladies – and work ceased at noon that Friday so they could be ready for the 4.30pm start. Younger workers were seated in the ground floor Cutting Room, with the larger number of older workers and visitors provided for in the Assembly Room. Employees from the firm's Burton Latimer branch were brought in by charabancs. After tea, speeches were made in the beflagged Assembly Room (above) led by society president William Walker, who chaired a large platform of VIP Co-operators. The firm had made £25,667 the previous year – six times the national average in the clothing industry – and cheques were presented to four surviving pioneers. In the evening the entire workforce trooped off to the Victoria Theatre in Gold Street for a performance of *Charley's Aunt*, followed by a dance to music played by the society's own orchestra, conducted by Walter Dyson, one of the tea organisers.

Long before the days of TV, radio and computer games, most leisure activities revolved around church and chapel, with parades, marching bands and tea-drinking much to the fore. This well-populated picture, taken during a typical Sunday School 'treat' circa 1908, shows one such procession reaching the Market Place after parading through the High Street. The 'treat' was one of the social highlights of the year involving virtually the whole town as organisers, participants or spectators. Weeks of preparation went into the success of the event, which included the massed singing of patriotic hymns on the Market Place followed by tea and refreshments for up to 4,000 children, usually in the Manor House Field. The parade, led by Parish Church pupils, would usually leave Dalkeith Place at 2pm, its roundabout route taking in Wellington Street and Rockingham Road to pick up those from other Sunday Schools. The youngsters, many carrying banners of identification, would then march back along Newland Street, Gold Street and High Street, led by bands and the town's rector, and cheered on by proud parents on the pavements. After tea, buttered bread and cakes, the children would make their way to North Park in Bath Road for sports, including the obligatory three-legged and egg-and-spoon races.

This unique view inside the Victoria Hall in Gold Street was taken at the old folks' tea party to celebrate the Coronation of King George V on Thursday 22 June, 1911. A total of 520 of the 555 guests invited – the oldest being a 90-year-old woman – sat down to tea. During the interval, council chairman Alfred Lewis presented everyone with a souvenir mug, followed by speeches from organising committee chairman Frank Mobbs, the Reverend C. B. Lucas (the rector) and the Reverend D. Stephens (Toller Church). Entertainment was provided by the Men's Own Band, Harry Mobbs with his gramophone, comedian Billy Eagle (see page 171) and the children of Rockingham Road School.

This curious photograph, taken on 19 May 1925, shows the climax to the annual Hospital Week in Kettering, when Lady Manningham-Buller launched a unique scheme to raise money by "mottoes". A grand total of £129 was paid by the public to have their own hospital "motto" chalked on the pavements of the town by dozens of artists, including William Blamire (pictured). Unfortunately a heavy rainstorm on Friday night made many pavements damp and difficult to write on, but all were completed. A total of 57 mottoes were sponsored and the town was divided into 17 districts, each with its own organiser. They included "SOS – Subscribe on Saturday", "Good health is better than wealth", "Your penny's a pill for those who are ill" and (outside the police station) "Beware of pickpockets – we want to pick yours – put a bob on the bobby!" A further £173 was raised by a house-to-house collection and money from passers-by thrown into strategically placed children's cots (used as collection boxes). Heavy rain soon washed the mottoes away but, fortunately, the coins remained on the pavement (how trusting they were in those days). And this was many decades before Red Nose Day!

There is so much to see in this marvellous photograph taken in Dalkeith Place circa 1911. It shows the gathering of bands, soldiers and organisations for a church parade, probably on Feast Sunday, held every year to mark the arrival of Kettering Feast. Events would include the ringing of church bells, thanksgiving services, music galore from town bands, and sports in aid of the hospital. In the morning there was the inevitable parade to the parish church by the Yeomanry, Territorials and people from all three emergency services. As seen here, the men assembled in Dalkeith Place before marching through Silver Street, Gold Street, High Street and Sheep Street, led by Drum-Major Rixon, wielding his handsome staff, and the Rifle Band under conductor Mr T. R. Preston. After the service the parade re-formed to march back to Dalkeith Place, where it was dismissed. On the right of the picture is the former Kettering Dairy in front of the Cross Keys Tavern (now O'Malleys pub) and the Parish Church School (in the distance). Coming back along the left side of the picture are the Liberal Club (now the Xtra pub) and leather merchants Staynes & Smith (now the Earl of Dalkeith). On the nearside left a mother and baby watch from the terrace above Robert Hall's basket and brush shop. Behind them is what appears to be a conservatory!

The whole nation took to the streets on Saturday 9 August 1902 to celebrate the Coronation of King Edward VII and his consort Queen Alexandra. Kettering's festivities were the biggest in the county outside Northampton involving virtually every organisation in the town. Urban council chairman Alfred Webb headed a 40-strong committee which took six months preparing the busy programme of events. Highlights included a grand parade through the town leaving from the cattle market in London Road at 10.30am (the fire brigade led by Captain Brewer is pictured (left) aboard its No. 1 engine going down Gold Street) and a huge open air tea party in Headlands (above), after 7,000 children aged 3 to 14 held their own procession. Tables and chairs were laid out on both sides, from the Sheep Street end to Sunnylands, home of shoe chief William Timpson (now St Peter's School). An army of 100 ladies had spent all morning preparing the food at the Corn Exchange on Market Place, with the tea 'brewed' in vast beer vats loaned by the Elworthy Brewery in Gold Street. Attendants were assigned to each table for the mammoth feast, which required 40 lbs of tea, 600 lbs of sugar, 190 lbs of butter, 21,170 lbs of bread and 2,968 lbs of cake!

The first chapter of my previous book, *20th Century Kettering*, began with a picture of a crowded High Street after the 1902 Coronation procession had passed. This splendid photograph, taken from the very same spot, shows what had been witnessed earlier. The parade was led by mounted members of the Northants Yeomanry, the town's Chief Constable, Supt Andrews (also on horseback) and the Rifle Band, under Tom Seddon. Then followed a cavalcade of horsemen, each representing a well-known personage. The lone rider in the picture, dressed in full Life Guardsman uniform, is the parade's chief marshal Trevor Spencer, whose portrayal of Tommy Atkins earned him first prize for best dressed horseman. The fire engine on page 70 was followed by three four-horse carriages, with council leaders in the first, the Local Board of Guardians in the second and the School Board in the last. Bringing up the rear was the Town Band, leading a procession of people in fancy dress and floral wagons and carts, decorated by local businesses, traders and organisations. Prizes of up to three shillings (15p) were given for the best floats and individuals. Winner of the best decorated building in the town was the Liberal Club. (*Tony Smith Collection*)

We move on now to the parade through the High Street to mark the Coronation of King George V and Queen Mary on Thursday 22 June, 1911. Despite inclement weather, the grand procession left the Cattle Market in London Road soon after 11am, its extended route taking in Hawthorn Road, Queensberry Road, Station Road and back up Bowling Green Road. This was at the request of Mr Sattin, master of the workhouse in London Road (now St Mary's Hospital), so that inmates could also enjoy the pageantry. After its success in the 1902 Coronation, a huge street party was again held in Headlands (left) and the entire length of Broadway. A total of 6,200 children sat down – 95 at each table – each receiving a souvenir mug (those unable to attend had mugs and cake taken to their homes). After tea, almost 600 youngsters entered sports held in a field off Headlands, but the programme ended early due to driving rain and was rescheduled for the following day. (*Tony Smith Collection*)

CORONATION of H.M. KING GEORGE V.
22nd June, 1911.

KETTERING CELEBRATION.

Children's Tea to be served in the Headlands and Broadway after the Children's Procession.

For Position of Tables see Street Map in Official Programme.

HELPER'S TICKET

Unprecedented scenes of rejoicing were witnessed in Kettering town centre when delayed peace celebrations were held on Saturday 19 July, 1919 to allow servicemen returning from the war to take part. One of the most moving events of the day was the gathering of thousands of people in the Manor House Field to see a performance by a massed choir of 500 voices, conducted by Sam Roughton. A massive morning parade was led by urban council chairman Lewis Richards, followed by the police, post office staff, VAD nurses, girl guides, with discharged and demobbed men and serving soldiers bringing up the rear.

The procession, pictured here in Gold Street (left and right) and Market Place (centre), also included mounted troops, the Town Band, Salvation Army Band, Rifle Band and Victoria Mission Band. Heavy rain forced the postponement of the sports programme until the Monday afternoon. Thousands of children were entertained to tea in their schools, there was music and jazz dancing on the Market Place and a Punch and Judy show on the Church Institute Field. Buildings were swathed in patriotic bunting, with some shops displaying wreaths as a mark of respect for those men who didn't return.

Kettering's famous "lido" is featured in the spectacular panoramic photograph above. The open-air swimming pool was part of the town's old baths in Bath Lane, opened in March 1915. Major modernisation of the outdoor pool and sunbathing terrace was included in a £4,000 scheme by the urban district council, which included a new filtration plant for the indoor pool. More than 700 people attended the re-opening ceremony on 9 July 1935, conducted by council chairman Charles Mayes, JP. Water improvements made it on a par with the town's drinking supply, new showers were installed and a new locker system was introduced for the protection of patrons' personal property and clothes. New cubicles were provided for the lido and bathers were given a numbered tag to fit to their costume, corresponding to that on the locker. The sunbathing terrace was for bathers to use after swimming, when they had changed out of their wet gear. It was designed to form a veritable sun-trap, tastefully decorated with hanging baskets. Other new features were a type of foot spray, operated by mere pressure of the foot, and custom-built footbaths outside the cubicles (unique at the time) to ensure every bather had to pass through it before entering the pool. Attendants were also given smart new all-white uniforms. The dates of the lido photographs are not known but the divers (left) are pictured in 1937.
(*Tony Smith Collection*)

At the turn of the last century Kettering was visited by a travelling circus, complete with performing animals, trapeze artists and novelty acts. This picture, taken around 1904, shows "Lord" George Sanger's show wagon at the top of Bowling Green Road. On the top of the wagon you can see a 'live' lion and a lamb with their trainer.

This Feast Day parade, pictured in High Street with Bakehouse Hill in the background, was taken by Spencer Percival on Sunday 4 July 1909. The parade through the town centre ended at the parish church for the 10am service. Members of the 4th Battalion Northants Regiment & Yeomanry, under the command of Major Fisher, were joined by members of the fire brigade, St John Ambulance and police. At the head of the procession Drum Major Rixon wielded his staff, followed by the Rifle Band, conducted by Mr T. R. Preston. After the service, the men returned to Dalkeith Place where the band played the National Anthem and all were dismissed.

Anyone living in Northampton Road (top left) or Greenhill Road (bottom) might recognise their house on this impressive aerial photograph of Kettering Feast taken on 10 July 1959. The picture shows how much of the old Recreation Ground the annual fair once took up with its rides, stalls, caravans and trailers before the site was dissected by the access road to Kettering Leisure Village. I would have been coming up to five years old when this was taken, so undoubtedly I would have visited the feast that week to have a go on the "Hook-a-Duck" (a prize every time) and the Hurricane Jets, introduced two years earlier. For more than a century the fair was synonymous with the Thurston family of showmen. The business was founded by the legendary Henry "Froggy" Thurston, the son of a Cambridge bricklayer, who bought a children's hand-operated street roundabout from a rag and bone merchant in 1868. The ride proved so popular at local school treats and fetes that he built a larger machine and left the brickyard to travel as a full-time showman attending feasts and fairs. In 1999 I wrote the obituary of Charles William Thurston, whose death marked the end of an era. It brought to an end the Thurston dynasty at Kettering Feast. Although the family name was retained, the fair continued to run under Norwich-based showman John Bugg. Charles's father John Henry was born at Kettering Feast in 1895 and his grandfather, also Charles, introduced the first moving pictures to Kettering people when he brought his famous bioscope to the town in 1901. A picture of this can be found on page 151 of my first book, *Kettering Revisited*. The inset picture, taken in the 1930s by radio pioneer Paul Taylor, shows Mr J. H. Norman on his popular "Spinner" stall at Kettering Feast. Note the money stacked on the record turntable.

Following growing interest in the scout movement in the early 20th century, Kettering's first scout parade was held on 11 July 1909. Its arrival at the parish church for the afternoon service was captured here by Spencer Percival, with the George Hotel in the background. The procession, headed by two giant banners (one seen here) and the Church Army Band, took in Rockingham Road, Regent Street, Wellington Street, Montagu Street, and High Street before reaching Sheep Street. The scout master was the Reverend B. T. D. Smith, curate of All Saints Church, and the service was conducted by the rector, Canon Patrick Smythe. Contingents of scouts from Desborough, Rothwell and Wellingborough also took part.

We would not approve today, but at the turn of the last century Kettering people were entertained by the annual visit of two travelling foreigners, believed to be either Russian or Hungarian, with a pair of tethered dancing bears. This photo was taken from the London Road end of The Grove, with the old St Edward's Church on the right. At the time Kettering people recalled what a noise the animals made when locked up overnight in the stables behind the Robin Hood pub in Northall Street.

This delightful scene shows children dancing around the Maypole in the playground of Stamford Road Infants School in the early 1900s. At that time there were two schools sharing the building, the infants and the mixed, with more than 600 pupils in the former and over 400 in the latter. (*Tony Smith Collection*)

This photograph, taken around the same time, shows children playing a musical game in the hall of Stamford Road School. The building, opened by the Right Hon A. H. Acland in 1892, was erected by Alfred Barlow to designs by John Alfred Gotch (see page 113). The premises are now used as a youth and education centre, named after the legendary Kettering missionary William Knibb. Both pictures were taken by Charles Speight. (*Tony Smith Collection*)

One of the pleasures in the "good old days" was the summer charabanc outing, usually local trips to the countryside or those stately homes open to the public. Sometimes day trips were made to seaside resorts on the east coast, such as Skegness, Hunstanton and Great Yarmouth (still popular with Kettering folk today). How weatherproof some of the vehicles were was another matter, although some had hoods which could be pulled over. This picture, taken in the 1930s, shows W. G. Keach's "luxury coach" outside the premises of leather firm G. H. Frecknall in Horsemarket. The Keach family were also coal merchants in Crown Street.

Readers who have my first book, *Kettering Revisited*, will be familiar with Lifeboat Day. Although landlocked, Kettering had close links with the National Lifeboat Institution and in the early 1900s a lifeboat would be paraded around the town once a year to raise funds for the service. The boat, pulled by six shire horses, would leave from the Market Place and end up at the furnace reservoir, off Rockingham Road (pictured), where children were given penny rides by crewmen.

This historic photograph was taken in the very early days of Wicksteed Park (before the meadow was mown) and when children's rides were pretty crude and didn't appear to be particularly safe (the "Giant Stride" is demonstrated by the youngsters here). When Charles Wicksteed bought pastureland near Barton Seagrave in 1911, his original idea was to develop a model village of more than 150 low-cost prefab houses with decent gardens, surrounding a large grass area and lake. But after the First World War, the lifting of building restrictions and the creation of the first council houses rendered his plans redundant, so he went ahead with a recreational park. Amazingly a small block of early prefabs survives on the Barton Seagrave side of the river, which are still lived in.

These three unique photographs show the early stages of the development of Wicksteed Park since it opened on 14 May 1921. It was not long before the need for refreshments became apparent and a wooden canteen (above right) was built in 1922, to be replaced the following year by the first pavilion (left), part of which is still incorporated today. The bandstand and the ever-popular water chute (top left) were built in 1926. The latter is still an attraction after recent refurbishment. (*Tony Smith and David Capps Collections*)

Eagle-eyed readers might spot the great Charles Wicksteed himself among the crowds at his playground in this picture from the 1920s. The much-loved philanthropist, seen here with his trademark bushy beard and walking stick, not only gave his park to the town but also made its playground equipment at his factory in Digby Street, which is still in operation. Temporary swings and see-saws were first put in the park for a Sunday School treat for workers at the factory. These were designed and made by Charles himself using bars and tubes which the plant produced for steam engines, but proved so successful that the idea was developed during the 1920s and a two-acre playground was built containing 70 playthings, all free of charge. Mr Wicksteed founded his engineering firm in 1876, five years after moving to Kettering from his native Leeds, and it began as a small workshop to repair Mr Wicksteed's ploughing machines. He also made tubing and other machinery, plus a nice sideline in bicycles. In 1928 he even invented an ingenious machine which could both slice and butter bread at an incredible 2,000 slices an hour. That was the same year that the park's cycle track opened and three years before its famous miniature railway was built – still the most popular attraction. Sadly Mr Wicksteed died in February 1931, before the project was completed. (*Tony Smith Collection*)

These men in their dapper uniforms, pictured during the August Bank Holiday of 1939, are not British naval officers but staff who once worked at the boathouse in Wicksteed Park, hiring out an assortment of rowing boats and pedaloes to the public. The building of the man-made lake, spanning 30 acres, began just before the First World War, to be completed afterwards. I've seen a marvellous cine film of the first regatta at the park taken shortly after it opened, attended by thousands, many of whom took to the water in home-made crafts, rafts and barrels. Sadly I've never come across photos or postcards of these in action – or not, as the case may be! The lake was formed from the original River Ise, the Nene's main tributary, which feeds the lake to this day. A moment of history is captured in the smaller picture – the building of the main bridge over the park lake which led to the boathouse and, later on, the water chute, the famous aviaries, the miniature cars and Pet's Corner. (*Tony Smith Collection*)

7. Trade and Commerce

This chapter takes a look at some of Kettering's best (and least) known businesses, shops, traders and pubs of yesteryear. We begin with one of the impressive premises owned by Arthur Richard Brake, the popular pawnbroker, jeweller, clothier and house furnisher. Owners of my previous books may remember the imposing facade of Brake's jewellery and pawn shop at the foot of Gold Street at its junction with Meeting Lane (formerly Moore's toyshop). This commanding corner was where Mr Brake, a native of Marston Trussell, near Market Harborough, established his first Kettering premises in 1887. He had learnt his trade working for a leading pawnbroker in Leicester and went on to manage his own business before moving to Kettering. In 1890 he acquired the neighbouring building known as Jenkinson's block in Meeting Lane (now opticians Dolland & Aitchison), where he built up a healthy trade selling household furniture Over the next 40 years he also ran a successful menswear shop in Montagu Street and a third branch on the corner of Regent Street and Wellington Street. This is almost certainly the only surviving picture of the Montagu Street store, which stood next to Henry Porch's confectioners (just visible on the right) and opposite the Central Hall entrance. The two assistants and the delivery boy are posing outside the premises, with proudly displayed price tags giving us a good idea how much of a bargain you got in 1910. The premises are now occupied by Esquires Barbers and the Mirror Image ladies' hairdressing salon.

Benjamin Calton was a popular butcher in Kettering for more than 30 years. Born in Suffolk, he set up his first pork butchery in Bedford before moving to Kettering in 1878. His first shop was in the High Street, but at the turn of the last century moved to more modern premises in Market Street, pictured here. Mr Calton was a regular at St Andrew's Church and outlived his wife and two children before succumbing to a six-month illness. He died, aged 83, at his London Road home in May 1932, when the business was continued by his nephew Mr H. C. Calton.

Draper and milliner Ernest Albert Hall died at Kettering General Hospital in March 1943, after collapsing a week earlier at his home in Market Place. Aged 72, he was born in Bristol but had lived in Kettering for 36 years. His first drapery was at No. 6 Market Street (where the Yorkshire Bank now stands) but, by the time he retired in 1923, his business was so successful that he also acquired Nos. 25 and 26 across the road, known locally as Hall's Corner. Mr Hall was a regular contributor of poems to the *Kettering Leader*, with some of his work appearing almost every week. He was a staunch Wesleyan and active member of the Central Methodist Church. He had two beloved sons – John was killed in the First World War and Henry lost his life in the London Blitz in the Second World War. He left a widow, Rose.

Henry Peter Hodge was a 'Jack of all trades' – a successful wholesale and retail plumber, glazier, decorator and electrical and gas engineer. He was also a successful builder and developer, credited with introducing incandescent light to Kettering and pioneering street lamps. After running his own business in Great Bowden from 1872 to 1892, Henry's first Kettering premises were in Lower Street near East's factory but three years later he built his own on the corner of Lower Street and Trafalgar Road. Designed by Gotch & Saunders, the building featured a distinctive illuminated clock which came on and off automatically. He came to the town in the midst of a building boom and carried out many large and important contracts for local public authorities. Henry acquired Kettering's first Edison phonograph and did a thriving trade in the new 'talking machines' long before music sellers took over the business. He was a deacon at Fuller Church, superintendent of the Fuller Children's Mission for 25 years and a pioneer of Kettering Eisteddfod.

Newman's ironmongers have been trading in Kettering for more than a century and must be one of the oldest family firms in the town. It was founded in 1900 by Harry Newman with the help of a £5 loan from a friend. An assistant is pictured outside the first premises in Montagu Street on the opposite side of the road to the present shop (since demolished to become the Swan pub's car park). The business transferred to its existing site in 1929, when Harry took over three premises, and, on his death during the Second World War, it was left to his three sons, Leonard, Percy and Edgar. The latter, who died in 1976 aged 71, served on Kettering Council for 22 years (until 1973), was the borough mayor in 1957-58 and made an Alderman. The shop became the main Calor Gas agent for Kettering and Corby and branched out to sell a wide range of DIY tools and garden machinery. It is now run by Harry's nephew Jim, son of Leonard.

Bridgnorth-born ironmonger Robert Bell, one of a family of 11, served his apprenticeship in the trade at Bamford's implement works in Utoxeter. His first business was set up in Market Harborough before establishing a branch at the bottom of Bakehouse Hill in Kettering in 1910. He closed the Harborough shop when he made Kettering his permanent home in 1914. Mr Bell built up a large clientele throughout the district and was well respected by the local farming industry. He was also a prominent member of St Edward's Church for 21 years, sang in its choir and was president of the Kettering branch of the Society of St Vincent de Paul. Robert was ill for a year before he died at his Warkton Lane home in March 1935, aged 63. Six months before his death he went into partnership with Arthur Billows, who eventually bought out Robert's daughters but retained the name Bell & Billows. Arthur had three sons, Colin, Bernard and John (who founded the plant hire company John R. Billows Ltd). Bernard stayed with his father in the Bakehouse Hill shop until it was demolished in 1969 – ironically, by John R. Billows! A superb colour photograph of the premises before they were pulled down was on the front jacket of my previous book, *20th Century Kettering*.

This picture (right), taken in 1908, shows the Montagu Street premises of the quality fish, game and poultry dealer Wilfred Mudd. By coincidence, Wilfred, like Mr Bell, was born in Bridgnorth, Shropshire, coming from a family associated with the fishing industry at Grimsby. He came to Kettering in 1895, opening his first shop in the High Street opposite Bakehouse Hill. In those times home deliveries were made by cart and cycle carriers, supplying everyone from the general public to the landed gentry and principal hotels. When this picture was taken both shops were running at the same time but the Montagu Street branch had closed by the beginning of The Great War. Mr Mudd was once chairman of the town's Chamber of Trade and treasurer of both the hospital sports and nursing social committees.

Early last century William Horden & Son's jeweller's shop stood on Bakehouse Hill between Allen's bakehouse and the Co-op's No. 1 store. An advert published in 1920 offers a variety of watches and clocks, made and repaired by William. But also on sale were early Meccano sets, model steam engines, clockwork trains and electrical apparatus – not to mention spectacles and eye-glasses from a shilling a pair! After marrying at Thrapston Parish Church in 1878, William lived with his wife in Lower Street and was a sidesman at Kettering Parish Church for 40 years. The couple had two sons – William Henry, who for many years ran his own watchmaking business in William Street, and Lance Corporal George, also a watchmaker and master craftsman, who worked with his father and was one of the founder members and secretary of the town branch of Toc H.

This 1908 picture shows the imposing frontage of the Newland Street grocery run by John William Baines. Before and during the First World War Mr Baines also had a branch store in Mill Road, managed by Samuel Webb. The Newland Street shop, taken over by T. A. Cobley in 1919, originally opened in 1886 as Hackett & Baines. Also known as the Public Supply Stores, the family grocers were also known for their hams and bacons. Early on they also specialised as tea and coffee merchants and in 1890 became wholesale agents for the Hop Tea Company of London. Their pure blend of Indian and Ceylon teas with the best Kentish hops was said to be medicinal and endorsed by *The Lancet* as an aid to digestion. The store also sold Gilby's wine and spirits, famous for their cowslip wine.

The Old Market Inn, which faces the Market Place today, has a long history going back to the 18th century. It was first known as The Saracen's Head Inn and in 1796, at the height of the woollen trade in Kettering, it became the venue for the town's yarn market, previously held at the former Duke's Arms pub in Market Street (pictured on page 12 of my book *Kettering Revisited*). The pub has gone through several name changes in the past two centuries When a Mr Fuller from London took over The Saracen's Head on 8 September 1815, he changed it to The New Inn, pictured here circa 1916. Standing outside is landlord Isaac Lee, who was mine host at the pub for more than 20 years. In more recent times it was also known as The Market Tavern before adopting its current monicker.

Two doors down to the left of The Old Market Inn is The Cherry Tree in Sheep Street, another local alehouse with origins going back hundreds of years. This picture was taken in 1906, when the licensee was Robert Augustus Manton, but it is said that alcohol has been sold on this site since the 17th century. Mr Manton was landlord for the early part of the last century but trade directories prior to 1903 list him as a beer retailer and do not mention the pub by name. Between The Cherry Tree and The New Inn in those days was where Ernest Woodcock began his drapery and millinery business in 1894 before moving to the corner of Newland Street and Montagu Street. From 1910 to 1988 the premises were occupied by Linnett's newsagents and the name is retained to this day. (*Tony Smith Collection*).

At this Depot there are about **100** BICYCLES to be sold from **10/-** each.

Montagu Street, Kettering.

H. TAYLOR

We do all kinds of CYCLE REPAIRS.

We build BICYCLES to order at **£8 10s. 0d.** with Eady, Lloyds, or B.S.A. Fittings. Dunlop or Palmer Tyres.

This commanding corner of Montagu Street and Silver Street was once Kettering's best-known bicycle shop. The business was founded by Harry Taylor in the 1890s, operating from small premises in Gas Street and High Street, but had the old Georgian house in Silver Street converted to a cycle shop at the same time as the opposite corner of the Gold Street crossroads was developed (see page 25). The house was for many years the home of wine and spirit merchant Robert Everett and later veterinary surgeon Trevor Spencer. When Harry Taylor died in August 1932, aged 71, the business was carried on by son Paul, who set up the first radio receiver in Kettering using a simple crystal set. Paul had begun selling radio apparatus from his father's shop ten years earlier and in 1938 he gave public demonstrations of television pictures for the first time in the town. He continued the Silver Street business until it was taken over by TV and electrical firm York & Sons in the 1960s.

The firm of A. W. Johnson sold fresh fruit and groceries to Kettering people for more than 50 years. Alfred William Johnson began as an errand boy to High Street fruiterer Mr Jacques and, when he was 19, he set up his own business in Regent Street, later moving to Market Place. Tragically he suffered heart problems and tubercular ulcers in his throat, dying in October 1910 aged just 37, leaving a wife and two sons. At his funeral a wreath in the shape of a heart was bought by fellow fruiterers and greengrocers. Walter Johnson, one of six brothers, took over the business which kept his name as a mark of respect. This picture was taken outside the shop on 7 March 1946, when a rare consignment of bananas arrived to be sold only to people under 18 in the Kettering and Corby area.

This photo from 1910 shows the George Street premises of George Tunnicliffe & Co, builders, decorators and sanitary engineers (plumbers). Mr Tunnicliffe came to Kettering from his native Staffordshire in 1893, starting out as a cabinet maker at various premises before settling in George Street. He had studied a Continental style of building after a trip abroad and built many houses and bungalows in the northern and eastern wards of the town. He was also an expert on antique china and furniture and served on the executive committee of Kettering Art Society for 15 years. George died, aged 59, in February 1924 after collapsing at work. The firm went into liquidation a year later.

With its Baroque balcony, spectacular 'Speight's Corner', at the junction of London Road and Bowling Green Road, has been one of Kettering's most striking landmarks since it was built to the designs of John Alfred Gotch in 1902. Charles Speight, who became the town's best-known photographer, came to Kettering from Rugby, setting up his first studio in Broadway. His wife Florence was the daughter of Edward Collings, owner of the Royal Hotel, and their own daughter Helen followed her father into the business which she continued after his death in February 1939. Charles kept abreast of all the latest developments in photography and was one of the first to introduce colour photography to the town. He was also a prominent Freemason and keen golfer and bowls player. Generations of local families sat for portraits at Speight's studios in the days when wedding pictures were taken there and not outside the church.

From 1946 until 1992 this distinctive corner of Horsemarket and Carrington Street was part of Dalkeith Ironmongers, founded by Frank Corvesor and Ernest Lillyman and continued after retirement by their respective sons Leo and Richard. But from late Victorian times until the 1920s the premises were occupied by James Foster, described in commercial directories as a "grindery dealer and seedsman" who also, judging by the picture, sold pet food and accessories. Old stables at the rear of the premises would have been well used in the 19th century for their original purpose but Dalkeith Ironmongers kept them as a storeroom.

This photograph, taken at the turn of the last century, shows the quality pork butcher's shop at No. 4 Lower Street, run for more than 50 years by George Harris. He established the business at around 1870 and sold every kind of fresh and cooked meats and tasty home-made pies and sausages. In the 1890s George was just one of 35 butchers working in Kettering. He later took over No. 3 Lower Street and added a branch at No. 4 Montagu Street just before the First World War. These were still going strong in the 1920s, but by the 1930s only the Montagu Street shop had survived, taken over by his sons. The shop on the right of the picture was owned by ironmonger Lewis Richards.

Many Kettering people will remember this Market Street newsagents and booksellers run by the family firm of J. Smith & Company. The business was established in 1895 by James Smith of Great Bowden as a newsagents and tobacconists, but later branched out into fancy goods and toys. At the rear of the shop there was also a large showroom selling everything from "pin cushions to perambulators" according to an old advertisement. In 1919 James was joined by his son Horace, who served as a Petty Officer during the First World War and took over the shop on his father's death in 1940. Horace, who lived in St Mary's Road, died in 1958, aged 64. Like Fred Moore, Horace took an interest in old Kettering and collected old books and antiques. He also told Fred his shop was haunted by the ghost of a drummer boy, one of a group of soldiers billeted at the 17th century Duke's Arms pub opposite (now long-gone). According to the tale, the young lad got into a fight and was murdered in an alleyway later incorporated into the shop. Fred said: "Horace never admitted to being a man who believed in ghosts but he reckoned he saw the boy shortly before he died. Horace often told friends he would sometimes sit at the back of the shop until late in the evening and when all was quiet he could hear the rat-a-tat-tat of a drummer." The premises later became a bicycle shop and now house the Perfect Inches Toning Studio.

Christopher Dixon's cobbler's shop was one of the last links with Kettering's shoemaking past. It stood at the top of the junction of Hazelwood Lane (left) and West Street (right) on the site of the 18th century Nag's Head Inn. In 1959 Kettering Council bought the derelict property for £975 in a clearance scheme and its ownership thwarted a controversial redevelopment scheme in 1966 which threatened the neighbouring Royal Hotel. The Royal's then owners, Watney Mann, drew up ambitious plans for 40 new shops, offices and a supermarket. It also wanted to build a brand new 800-room hotel which would have swept away not only the Royal but also the nearby Midland Bank. The proposal never got off the ground because the council's plot of land in West Street was crucial to the brewers' development, and the authority stood its ground (one its better investments, one might say). The old shop was eventually pulled down in 1972 and is now waste ground. Historically West Street was first called Dyker's Lane, then Nag's Head Lane (after the pub), before it was re-christened Mr Lamb's Lane in the early 1800s (after the well-known Lamb family). For five generations, since Napoleonic times, there has been a Mr Lamb practising as a solicitor at the bottom of West Street, where the Kettering office of Lamb & Holmes stands to this day. (*Tony Smith Collection*).

8. Kettering Buildings

This is a rare early photograph of the former Congregational Church (now United Reformed) standing proudly in isolation on the corner of London Road and St Peter's Avenue. The church was officially opened and dedicated on Thursday 4 May 1899, seven years after splitting from the town's Toller Chapel in Gold Street. The splinter group held its first service in the Temperance Hall in Gold Street on 6 November 1892 and a week later a Sunday School was established at the British Schools in School Lane (now the Four Seasons Day Centre). Services switched to the new Stamford Road School in 1894 but as this building was only available on Sundays and one weekday evening, the church acquired a new hall in the Post Office arcade (dubbed "the tin tabernacle") and furnished it with 200 comfy armchairs and a creaky harmonium (nicknamed "the old growler"). A fund set up to buy land and erect a proper church, with vestries and a lecture hall, raised £6,300. The new building was designed by architect H. A. Cooper and on 10 June 1898 hundreds of people witnessed the laying of foundation stones by the Reverend W. L. Lee (the church minister), the Reverend A. Rowland (Congregational Union chairman) and local businessman John Turner Stockburn (the church's first treasurer). In its formative years the church had a Mutual Debating Society, a ladies' group called The Women's Hour, a Christian Band and a Band of Hope. The Men's Conference held its first session in 1919 and The Women's Social Circle began in 1933. During the Second World War the church embarked upon a new venture when a Church For Little People was established at the Henry Gotch School. It began on 3 January 1943 to cater for very young children living on the newly developed Windmill Avenue estate, who found the walk to London Road was too long. Long-serving ministers at London Road Congregational have included the Reverend Charles Deeble (1912–1932), after whom a Kettering road was named, and the Reverend Leonard Wide (1933–1952), who died in 1981. (*Tony Smith Collection*)

The George Hotel in Sheep Street, pictured here in 1878, is believed to have been built on the site of the 18th century Cock Inn, although a date stone found in a wall during alterations in 1925 was inscribed "S L 1639". The 1920s revamp included a new dining room, the previous one was converted into a tea lounge and the former stables were turned into garages for 100 cars, with lock-ups and petrol pumps. Rooms bore distinctive names – The House of Commons, The House of Lords and The Devil's Kitchen (aka The Froth-Blower's Retreat). Over the entrance to the lobby were the words: "No peeresses served here!" In Victorian days Robert Harradine was the host for 40 years until Robert Marsh Everett, a former wine merchant in Market Street, took over in 1883. When he died in 1916 he was – at 77 – the town's oldest licensee. He died from internal injuries after slipping on snow and breaking a leg while walking to work from his Headlands home.
(*Tony Smith Collection*)

The Sun Hotel in Market Street, boasting 12 guest rooms, stood on the site where the famous missionary William Knibb was born in 1803. Last orders were called on 28 June 1960, when the property was disposed of by Phipps, the Northampton brewery. "There was no formal farewell gathering," said the *Evening Telegraph*, "The regulars, with accompanying reminiscences and guesses on what was and will be, held a small party of their own – and then the Sun went down. Perhaps it was coincidental that the two-year-old terrier Topper, owned by manager Walter Charsley, was off his usual drop of beer."

The Golden Lion pub on the left (later The Gaiety and now Watercress Harry's) introduced skiffle music to Kettering in 1957. Manager William Herbert Watkins booked a band one Friday night which was such a hit with young people they played two nights running the following week, but then ended after complaints by older customers!

This aerial picture of Kettering Parish Church (right) is unusual for two reasons. Firstly it shows the rarely-photographed east side of the church, but more interestingly, it shows a considerably larger graveyard extending back to London Road. The story behind this began in January 1951, when the *Evening Telegraph* ran a leader article urging the borough council to use part of the church cemetery to create a 'garden of rest' as a tribute to local men killed in the Second World War. The paper suggested such a scheme would be an ideal contribution by the town towards the Festival of Britain celebrations being held that year. But what started out as an honourable and simple enough plan developed into a saga which took almost a decade of wrangling before coming to fruition. The *Evening Telegraph* argued that the view of the church would be improved and sponsorship by local firms and individuals would minimise any cost to the ratepayer. The idea was backed by Kettering rector, Canon Holborow, and discussed at a public meeting, but one of the stumbling blocks was the borough council's inability to spend public money on land it didn't own. And although the church council was willing to let the local authority convert the graveyard, it was reluctant to give up the freehold of the land. There was also concern about the removal of tombstones, some dating back to the 18th century. The deadlock lasted almost a decade until a compromise was reached, whereby the council was granted a 99-year lease of the land at a nominal rent and the gravestones affected were re-erected around the walls of the new garden. Several memorial seats were donated by townspeople and the garden of rest was finally opened in September 1960 by the Bishop of Peterborough, the Right Reverend Robert Stopford. The Victorian view of the church (above) shows its southern side with grass covering the site which later became the cattle market and is now the London Road car park. (*Tony Smith Collection*)

Now here's a real collector's item and the only one I've ever seen – a postcard of Kettering's old police station in London Road produced by the Excelsior Patent Stone Company to advertise the quality of its work. The original building was erected in 1851, enlarged in 1894 and extended again in 1909, when this card was published. It was used to acknowledge receipt of a customer's written enquiry, order or complaint, and to assure the person that the matter was being given immediate attention. In 1909 the premises were modified and partly rebuilt by local contractor Mr O. P. Drever (see page 56) to designs by county surveyor Mr C. S. Morris. The frontage was typically early Victorian in style and the ground floor included two courts for Petty Sessions, two replacement cells, a guard room, witnesses' room, magistrates' retiring room and kitchen. There was also an inspector's house, with men's quarters upstairs.

This fading photograph taken by Spencer Percival is probably the only record of the official opening of the police station extensions on Wednesday 11 August 1909. A large crowd assembled in London Road at 10.30am to witness the ceremony, performed by county council chairman Colonel S. G. Stopford-Sackville. All 30 town constables and four sergeants were also present in their new white summer hats, under the command of Superintendent William Gabriel Hooper and Inspector Tebbey. At 10.45am exactly – captured here on camera – Mr Stopford-Sackville carried out the symbolic opening of the station gates with a silver key bearing an engraving of the county rose on its handle. The Justices then entered the courtroom, where their chairman John Turner Stockburn made a speech and proposed a vote of thanks to Mr Stopford-Sackville. The constables were then inspected in the exercise yard behind the station.

This rare photograph of Kettering's original fire station (above) was taken circa 1903. The building stood near the top of Market Street opposite the Boys National School (later Parish Church School) in Horsemarket – on the site later occupied by the old weights and measures department. Station Officer Bruxby is pictured with the No. 1 and No. 2 steamers, made by Shand Mason of London and provided by the Local Board. No. 1 engine (left) was capable of pumping 260 gallons a minute but No. 2 (right) could handle 450 gallons a minute and had a fire escape ladder which extended to 55 ft. The steamers were pulled by horses stabled at the Royal Hotel. Mr Bruxby lived in a house next to the station and it was his job to ring for the horses, send the alarm out to the part-time firemen and get the hose cart ready for the first men to arrive. All the men were volunteers and their speed of turn-out became legend. It wasn't until 1919 that the brigade acquired a No. 1 Dennis motor engine (kept in Robinson's garage in Montagu Street) and it was another seven years before the rickety station was replaced by a smart new building lower down Market Street (now housing the Oasis Centre and Citizen's Advice Bureau). The premises included a hose drying and drill tower (pictured right), a workshop, recreation room and bathroom.

Now you see it, now you don't! Since the days when it was known as Goosepasture Lane, Meadow Road had always been a narrow road flanked by old cottages. This all changed in January 1960 when buildings opposite the Talbot Hotel and lower down on the same side of the street were pulled down for road widening. When the main photograph was taken, the properties on the left – opposite the gates of the Talbot, then run by Fred and Doris Hefford – had long been empty, awaiting demolition. The offices of solicitors Wilson Browne now occupy this site. One unoccupied house (see smaller picture) was 'sliced' from the end of the row of terraced homes known as New Cottages. Some occupants of the doomed cottages in Meadow Road were re-housed on the Piper's Hill and Weekly Glebe estates. The council had intended to widen the rest of Meadow Road as far as High Street, but didn't own the properties from the Granada car park upwards. Other ideas considered for developing the area included building old people's bungalows, a new art gallery, school, nursing home, a civic centre and a new town hall.

This is a bird's eye view of my spiritual home – Rockingham Road, headquarters of Kettering Town Football Club for more than 100 years. The Poppies' first ground was at Eldred's Field off School Lane (see page 12), followed by a short spell at North Park, then quite a sports arena with cycle and running tracks. Rockingham Road was previously used by Kettering Hawks and the footpath from Glendon Bridge and Second Lodge field to "Plank" Valley Walk passed across the pitch. It is said that when Leicester Fosse played the Poppies, the train stopped at the furnaces, the team jumped off and walked across to the ground! The inaugural match on 4 September 1897 was a 3-0 defeat by Ilkeston in the Midland League, attended by a crowd of 2,000. The old wooden grandstand at the top of the ground was opened on Boxing Day, 1924 when 4,267 fans saw the Poppies beat Northampton Reserves 2-0. The next milestone came in 1946 when the ground's notorious sloping pitch was levelled. More than 11,500 tons of soil were removed, the familiar "chicken run" disappeared and the stand from Kettering Town Cricket Club ground was erected in its place. Other improvements included new fences and railings, building banks for spectators and a car park. The railings at the Athletic Club end were rescued from a dump in Essex and concrete slabs came from demolished air raid shelters. The operation cost £2,500, paid for after a public appeal to the town's sportsmen. More than 3,200 supporters witnessed the official opening by national sports writer Peter Wilson on 16 September, when a thrilling friendly against the Metropolitan Police ended 5-5. The 1952–53 season saw the start of a football pool by the supporters' club, which raised £12,000 to build new dressing rooms. In 1954 new terracing was installed behind the Cowper Street goal using 600 tons of rubble, 600 concrete curbs and 800 concrete slabs. Most of the work was done by groundsman George Robinson, who also rolled 100 tons of manure into the pitch and re-turfed the goalmouths. The first match I saw was the 2-2 draw with Alf Ramsey's Ipswich side on Monday 9 October 1961 when FA secretary Sir Stanley Rous officially switched on the new £11,000 floodlights. The picture here was taken the following year before construction of the new wall, canteen and clubhouse at the Cowper Street end, again paid for by supporters. The next major revamp came in the 1970s when a new £150,000 grandstand replaced the two rickety wooden ones. The photograph also shows the former ramshackle Tin Hat Club, behind the goal on the right, which became a leading venue for top rock and blues bands in the late 1960s.
(*Tony Smith Collection*)

These photographs are taken from a small booklet produced in 1937 to mark the Golden Jubilee of Kettering Working Men's Club. They show four of the impressive rooms at its Wellington Street premises – the refreshment bar (top left), billiards hall (top right), cinema and concert hall (bottom left) and the library (bottom right). Indoor games provided on the premises ranged from darts and dominoes to cards, chess and table skittles. There was a separate room with four tables for billiards and snooker, while outdoor pursuits included bowls and fishing. The library stocked 2,000 books, which members could borrow free for a fortnight, but there was a penny charge if returned late. Daily and weekly papers and magazines were also provided in the reading room. Cinema shows were held every Saturday and Sunday in the concert hall, which seated up to 500, with dances and shows held most Fridays. Bathrooms were available with a fourpenny fee for use of a towel, but a wash and brush-up was free of charge. The brochure does not give the membership fee but a Mutual Aid Society was formed to help any member in distress, through no fault of their own, such as illness or accident. This cost sixpence per week, with sick pay at a rate of twelve shillings per week and six shillings weekly for the next six. The club also ran an old age pension fund, which made weekly payments plus a Christmas box each year. Club rules for members were: 1. To promote sobriety and sociability: 2. To be proud of the club and make it something to be proud of: 3. To be courteous and cultivate self-respect: and 4. To take part in the work of the club, to not only be clubmen but gentlemen. Members were also forbidden to gamble or pass betting slips on the premises. The Wellington Street club (now Kettering Sports & Leisure Club), opened in August 1921, having previously been based at a disused factory in Meadow Road. (*Tony Smith Collection*)

Stamford ~ Road Schools, for the
KETTERING SCHOOL ~ BOARD.

Gotch & Saunders
Architects: 1891.

This drawing was the original artist's impression of the Stamford Road Schools drawn up by local architects Gotch & Saunders in 1891, complete with a diagram of the interior. In 1870 the government passed the Elementary Education Act allowing towns with church-run schools to build new non-denominational schools to cope with any extra demand for pupil placements, and a School Board to administer them. At that time Kettering already had four church (National) schools and one non-conformist (British) school but there were so many unplaced children by 1890 that Whitehall insisted that the town complied. Stamford Road Schools, built by Alfred Barlow, were subsequently commissioned by the newly-elected Board and officially opened in December 1892, with Mr J. J. Rawson as its first headmaster (see page 180).

This postcard from the early 1900s shows the exterior and rarely seen interior of the Carey Mission House in Lower Street. It was here that the Baptist Missionary Society was formed in 1792 at a meeting in the parlour of Martha Wallis, who lived there and after whom the old people's flats behind the building were named in 1979. Among those at that first select meeting were local minister, the Reverend Andrew Fuller, and the group's first missionary William Carey, both of whom are remembered in the names of two Baptist churches in the town. For many years the striking seven-bayed building, with its Collyweston slate roof, was the home of the legendary John Turner Stockburn, who had a corset factory in nearby Northall Street and was a pioneer of the town's Local Board, School Board, water company and general hospital. The Mission House today houses flats for the elderly.
(*Tony Smith Collection*)

This historic cottage in Hazelwood Lane became the birthplace of non-conformity in Kettering in 1662, when protestant dissenters held their first meetings there. They gathered in the wake of the Reverend John Maidwell's ejection from Kettering Parish Church, where he had been rector for the previous 11 years. Secret meetings were held at houses in other parts of the town but most took place in this quaint old stone farmhouse, probably because it was occupied by Mr Maidwell's grand-daughter, Mrs Hazelwood. Three centuries later the property was in such a poor state that it was demolished in October 1956, despite being deemed of great historical and architectural interest. A suggestion that some stones of the building should be used to erect a memorial marking the site was not taken up by the council, but Toller Church and Fuller Church each chose a piece of stone to keep as a memento. This photograph was taken by Herbert Winterhalder (see page 166), who signed the front and back of the card on which it was mounted. (*Tony Smith Collection*)

Kettering Library in Sheep Street celebrates its centenary next year and this is the best quality photograph I have seen of its official opening on Saturday 7 May, 1904. Unusually, the ceremony was performed personally by Andrew Carnegie, its multi-millionaire benefactor, who met the bill of £8,450. He is the white-bearded gentleman in the centre of the picture on the arm of Mrs Mobbs, wife of urban council chairman Frank Mobbs behind her. The man with the brolly is Mr Mobbs' deputy Sam Taylor, standing in front of John Turner Stockburn, also with a white beard. The first book borrowed, issued and stamped by Mr Carnegie, was his own publication appropriately called *The Gospel of Wealth*! Mr Mobbs then presented him with a specially inscribed copy of F. W. Bull's *History of Kettering*. After signing the visitors' book, Mr Carnegie was driven, amid cheers, to the general hospital for a guided tour. He then visited the Stamford Road Schools before attending the official 'switch on' of the town's new electricity works and refuse destructor in Rockingham Road.

This picture, taken at the top of Station Road, appeared on a postcard stamped 15 June 1904. It shows just some of the huge crowd which gathered for the opening of the library, seen in the distance. Estimates of the crowd varied between 10,000 and 15,000 at a time when Kettering's population was around 30,000. The impressive red-bricked gabled building, with its mullioned windows and a pretty little cupola on top, was designed by Leicester architects Goddard, Paget & Catlow and erected by Kettering Co-operative builders. Although it could accommodate up to 30,000 books on its shelves, it began with around 6,000. My crumbling copy of the souvenir booklet published for the opening features a ground floor plan of the building, including both lending and reference libraries, a special section for rare books and separate reading rooms for newspapers and magazines.

This picture of the Midland Band Club in Hallwood Road was taken in 1914 before the Timpson factory dominated the skyline and when the building was used as the headquarters of the Scottish Horse Regiment (see page 40). The club, founded in 1897, was built on land previously known as Weekley Hall Wood and during the First World War its secretary was Arthur T. Smith, with Isaac Lee as steward. In those days there was an outdoor beerhouse on the ground floor selling Phipps ales from Northampton (later Watneys). The corner entrance was later bricked up and moved to the side facing Rockingham Road Pleasure Park and today there is a different frontage. The club car park and a private house now stand to the right of the building. Whether the club actually had a band is unclear as no records survive. Between the wars the Midland was a hotbed for top-class snooker, with the legendary local champion Jack Old as one of its star players. In 1926–1927 the club won the Kettering Amateur Billiards Championship and the National 'Club' Snooker Tournament, but its best season was 1935–1936 when it won six local and national trophies, including the All England Championships in both billiards and snooker. In later years it became better known for its bowls club, formed in 1952, with home matches played on the park green across the road. In its earlier days the club had a somewhat cliquey reputation with a long waiting list to become a member. This area was once considered a posh end of town, nicknamed "Rice Pudding Alley" by other working men's clubs. In the 1930s it had around 200 members compared with the current 900.

The Peacock

This was the original Peacock Inn in Lower Street shortly before it was demolished and rebuilt in 1960 by brewers Bass of Burton-on-Trent, its last licensee before closure being Lionel Wayman-Smart. The old Peacock, with its saloon bar, smoke room and off-licence, was popular with postmen after finishing their morning rounds. Early last century artistes performing at the nearby Victoria Hall in Gold Street would often stay there and at panto time young Kettering "blades" would flock to the bar to catch a glimpse of the leading ladies. William Sculthorpe, the licensee from 1895 to 1917, was once left with a tribe of performing pygmies, complete with loincloths, when their manager ran off at the end of the week after drawing their pay. The bemused publican fixed them up with a temporary home in the loft of the stables, where they lived under the scrutiny of townsfolk until other arrangements could be made. It was Mr Sculthorpe who put in the green and red tiled front of the building because he thought the former frontage was too drab and completely unlike a Peacock. One of the oldest records of the Peacock was dated 1833, but it was thought there was an inn on that site back in the 18th century. (*Tony Smith Collection*)

This photograph of The Odeon in Gold Street was taken the year before it closed as a cinema on Saturday 9 October 1960. It was built from the shell of the former Victoria Picture House by local contractors O. P. Drever & Son. My own mementoes include one of its original 'exit' signs and the souvenir programme for its grand opening on 19 September 1936. This was performed by Stephen Schilizzi, president of Kettering General Hospital, which also benefited from a collection taken before the main feature, '*Strike Me Pink*', starring Eddie Cantor. It cost Odeon Theatres £50,000 for the takeover, of which £15,000 funded major alterations, including the removal of the balcony, the building of a new 'circle' in its place and a complete revamp of the exterior. Seating more than 1,000, it became the town's busiest cinema with huge queues often tailing back down Bakehouse Hill. Shows were continuous after 2pm, with three performances on Saturday. In June 1946 the Odeon was the first cinema to appoint its own padre under a pioneering Christian scheme to help children with practical and spiritual problems. The Reverend John Rowe, minister of Woodford and Broughton Baptist Churches, had the use of the manager's office each Saturday morning, when kids enjoyed the adventures of *Flash Gordon*. Between 700 and 800 children aged 4 to 14 flocked to the Mickey Mouse Club every week, which had members' badges and even a club song! It was a sad day when the Odeon chain, owned by the Rank Organisation, succumbed to the trend of replacing old cinemas with new bingo halls. The curtain came down for good on 29 October 1960 after the final screening of the Norman Wisdom comedy *There Was a Crooked Man*, ending 72 years of entertainment on the site. Bingo lasted from 1961 to 1972 but the building was demolished two years later to make way for the Newborough Centre.

SAVOY THEATRE
RUSSELL STREET KETTERING

The Savoy in Russell Street opened as a cinema and theatre on Saturday 21 May 1938, rising from the ashes of a disastrous fire which gutted the former Coliseum, where the stars of music hall had once trod the boards. Although the plush art deco building was designed by Mr C. Edmund Wilford of Leicester and erected by contractors Leighton of London, many local firms were involved in its construction. Kettering Sand & Gravel Company supplied the plasterwork, Luck and Andrew provided the timber, A. G. Miller did the plumbing and Montagu Wallpaper & Paint Company supplied just what it said on the tin! It could seat up to 1,131, including 774 in the stalls, and the auditorium was modelled in relief plaster mouldings, with large Grecian garden murals each side of the proscenium. There were also seven dressing rooms and a separate one for the orchestra. The official opening by council chairman Walter Dyson was one of the events of the year, with souvenir programmes given to every invited guest. The main feature was *Big City*, preceded by the Pathetone weekly newsreel and a *Popeye* cartoon. Many still remember the popular Sunday night shows in the 1940s and 1950s with stars ranging from Ted Ray, Tommy Trinder and Arthur Askey to Sandy Powell, Dickie Murdoch and the cast of the legendary radio show ITMA. Big dance bands of the era also performed concerts. The Savoy hosted local operatic and theatrical productions and, at one time, weekly plays were staged by the Northampton 'Rep'. *Bonnie and Clyde* was the final film screened before the stalls were converted into a bingo hall and the circle into a smaller cinema with just 465 seats. *The Charge of the Light Brigade* was screened at the official opening of the new-look cinema by Kettering mayor Alderman Bob Denney on 29 September 1968. It was all-change again in 1973 when this was divided into two studio-style cinemas but dwindling audiences forced these to close in July 1984, leaving the town no cinema for the first time since 1910. It was back in business by Easter 1986 thanks to local entrepreneur and film buff Ashley Wyatt, who renamed it 'The Ohio' after Kettering's American twin-town. But when Odeon announced plans for an eight-screen luxury multiplex cinema, Mr Wyatt waved the white flag, closing a few months before the new complex opened in Pegasus Court on 11 December 1997. The building was awaiting demolition to make way for flats as this was written.

"Sunnylands" (left) was a Jacobean-style mansion in Headlands designed by John Gotch and the home of Kettering shoe firm giant William Timpson. He had it built in 1894 for his wife Elizabeth but sadly she never lived there, dying suddenly aged just 41. Shortly afterwards William married Katharine Mursell, whose father was a former minister of Fuller Church, and William continued to live there until his death in 1929. The house, with its four acres of grounds, was the wartime home of the Baptist Missionary Society before becoming St Peter's School, a mixed preparatory school for children aged 4 to 12. When it opened in May 1946, its first headmistress was Miss Joyce Rutherford, who had been women's secretary of the Baptist Missionary Society since 1931 and was the daughter of a former Lord Mayor of Liverpool. The school began with 50 children and three staff, but by the time it celebrated its Golden Jubilee in 1996, the roll call was 175 pupils, 29 teachers and 13 domestic staff. This picture was on a postcard sent by William Timpson to one of his Manchester shops on 20 March 1910.

This magnificent building (right) in Hall Lane, built in 1903 and extended in 1967, was originally "Bryn Hafod", stately home of legendary leisure park founder Charles Wicksteed. After his death in 1931, it was rented to Mr Mitchell, manager at Stewarts and Lloyds in Corby, before becoming the Convent of Our Lady in 1936. Today this quiet complex can accommodate up to 29 sisters in their own simply furnished rooms, many of which overlook beautiful gardens and have spectacular views of the town. The Congregation of the Sisters of Our Lady (known nationally as the Sisters of Notre Dame) is a worldwide apostolic institute founded in 1850. Its mother house is in Rome and its 2,500 sisters work in houses on every continent except Australia. The community, which lives under strict vows of poverty, chastity and obedience, began in Germany, came to England in 1933 and established its first convent at Hoddesdon, Herts, which still thrives. The Kettering convent has its own language school, where it teaches English to visiting sisters from America, Brazil, Korea and Indonesia. The preparatory school next door, set up by Ursuline sisters in 1936, has been owned by the Sisters of Our Lady since 1954 but closed only this year because of falling rolls.
(*Tony Smith Collection*)

When I was a young boy living in Valley Walk in the late 1950s, the field running down to the Ise brook was our playground. Near the bridge which crossed the brook towards what later became the Ise Village was this derelict and vandalised mill house (now long gone), which everyone reckoned was haunted! The old watermill at the end of its garden was taken down in 1895. Local children played in an open-air bath fed by the Ise, but the structure collapsed in the gale and blizzard of 1916. In the First World War army mules were kept in the old stables of the house, which was still lived in until the early 1950s.

Queen Street

What goes up must come down – at least that was Kettering Council's motto when it embarked on a slum clearance programme in the 1950s and 1960s. This picture from October 1958 shows the north side of Queen Street being torn down, houses numbered 17 to 59 to be precise. Land released by the demolition was used to widen what was one of Kettering's narrowest streets and today the site, occupied by the Ultra Bodies Gym and the Carrington Cars compound, is totally unrecognisable. Also swept away as part of the same radical programme were whole rows of former homes in St Andrew's Street, Northall Street, Job's Yard and Freestone Row (off Dalkeith Place).

Northall Street

It's the turn of Northall Street in this picture as more buildings bite the dust, including several houses and the old Spring Gardens pub – a proper photograph of which has so far eluded this collector! The eventual compulsory purchase of numerous other properties at the top end of the street – including Jack Cross's newsagents and buildings opposite – allowed the borough council to construct the inner-ring road in the 1970s
(*Tony Smith Collection*)

This photograph, taken in February 1925 by Lindsay Street builders Lewin & Son, shows preliminary shoring work next to Boots the Chemist prior to the construction of the new Westminster Bank in Market Place. Built of cold grey Portland stone, it was one of the earliest metropolitan buildings in the town. Kettering's first Boots branch was built on the corner of Market Street in the mid-1890s, where it remained until 1961, moving first to High Street and later its present site in the Newlands centre. The original shop and the Westminster Bank were both demolished in the 1970s and the site is now occupied by Barclays Bank.

This was the dangerous dog-leg in Market Street in January 1923 just before the demolition of Althorp's Fried Fish and Oyster Bar to widen the road. Part of the premises was previously used as a butcher's with its own stables and slaughterhouse at the rear. In the distance are yeast merchants Bishop & Brooke and Elizabeth Wallis's sweet shop (now an Indian takeaway). The Sun Hotel (see page 98) is on the right. (*Tony Smith Collection*).

The old British Legion Hall

On page 96 of my book *20th Century Kettering* is a colour photograph of the old British Legion Hall in Richard Leys when it was still being used in the 1960s. These two pictures were taken just before the corrugated iron building was pulled down in 1975 when the site was needed for the new Sainsburys store in the Newborough Centre. The left picture shows committee members taking a last wistful look at the "iron lady" who had served them well since 1947, when the former billiards saloon was transformed into a meeting place, dance and concert hall. It was the Legion's first permanent headquarters since the branch was formed at a meeting of ex-servicemen at the George Hotel 26 years earlier. A smart new club was incorporated into the Newborough Centre.

The Lawns

The Lawns (right), a three-storey house at the bottom of George Street, was once the home of the Loake family of footwear fame. In 1943 Ernest Loake gave it to the town as a youth centre, used by several local groups such the Air Training Corps and Sea Cadets. It had two large furnished recreation rooms with books, table games and a radio donated by townspeople. One room also had a billiards table. On the first floor were ATC instruction rooms, including a Morse and signals room fitted with 30 tapping keys and earphones, and an aircraft recognition room. An outside garage was used to teach mechanics and the ground floor had a cafe open from 9am to 10pm, which proved popular with out-of-town cadets who enjoyed tea and low-cost meals on parade nights. The building was demolished in December 1955 and its name has been adopted by the present-day council-run old people's complex in Saunders Close.

Manor House

The Manor House (left) in Sheep Street, with its Georgian facade, dates from the 18th century with some 17th century features. It is thought to stand on the site of the noble hall occupied by the Abbots of Peterborough in the Middle Ages. It was once the home of the Sawyer family and later Mr Eland, a local banker who kept peacocks. For some years last century it was used by the public health department, before the former school in Bowling Green Road was converted to council offices in 1965. The property then lay empty for two years while its future was under review. Although there was woodworm in some of the crossbeams, the building was basically sound. After a public meeting, it was decided to transfer the library's reading room to the ground floor and hire other rooms to local societies for meetings and coffee mornings. It has served as the town's excellent museum since 1989.

The Empire

Alas not even Fred Moore had a photograph of the old Empire in Eskdaill Street in its heyday as a picture house. It was the last cinema in Kettering to change over to 'talkies' in 1931 and its small auditorium could seat only 500, with 100 in the balcony (complete with double 'hugging hutches' at the back). But its grand Roman-style arched entrance and plush red seats inside gave it a certain character when it opened on 3 May 1920. Its manager was Montagu Street photographic dealer Harry Bamford, co-owner with Mr H. G. Roughton and Mr A. Cheaney until 1937, when the business was bought by Jack Sherwood, who then ran The New Coliseum in Russell Street. It changed hands twice more in the early 1950s, by then calling itself The New Empire after a major facelift and installing the most up-to-date sound and projection equipment. But dwindling audiences let to its closure on 19 June 1954, its last double feature being *Santa Fe* starring Randolph Scott and *Captive Girl* with Johnny Weissmuller. Today it is occupied by the Selecta Tyre and Exhaust Centre.

The Regal

The Regal (left), built on the site of Goosey & Sons' drapery store in High Street, was officially opened by Earl Spencer on Boxing Day 1936. This vast £70,000 super-cinema had a unique frontage dominated by a tower lit by a neon halo visible for miles around. Five pairs of entrance doors led into a large foyer with a pay desk on each side (both in use on busy weekends). The elegant air-conditioned ultra-modern auditorium, pictured here, had 2,000 luxury seats – grey in the stalls and blue in the circle. The 50ft wide stage, with footlights and an orchestra pit, boasted an elaborate frilly curtain, seen here draped in one of its 59 different patterns. This was used for popular Sunday night band shows with top names like Joe Loss, Jack Hylton, Henry Hall and Nat Gonella. Other stars included singers Anne Zeigler and Webster Booth, pianists Rawicz & Landaur, the legendary Flanagan and Allan and forces' sweetheart Vera Lynn in her prime. One of the early films shown at the Regal was *Queen of Hearts* starring Gracie Fields and the classic *Gone with the Wind* played for two weeks – unheard of in the provinces. (*David Capps Collection*)

On New Years Day 1948 The Regal was taken over by Granada Theatres and renamed The Granada, but, with no closure or major redecoration, it was business as usual although staff were kitted out in smart new uniforms. In the early 1950s the American craze for new three-dimensional films came to Kettering, with audiences wearing special spectacles to watch 3D versions of *Bwana Devil* and the Vincent Price horror flick *House of Wax*. This passing fad was followed by the installation of Cinemascope in September 1954, complete with a vast 52ft wide and 20ft high screen and four-track stereophonic sound. Being only a month old at the time, this writer didn't appreciate what an innovation this was! I did get excited, though, when the 'pop' package tours came to The Granada in the Swinging Sixties, when little Kettering was entertained by such stars as Gene Vincent, Little Richard, Billy Fury, Dusty Springfield, The Who and The Rolling Stones – sadly The Beatles went to the ABC at Northampton. But it was at The Granada that I saw the Fab Four films *A Hard Day's Night*, *Help!*, *Yellow Submarine* and *Let It Be*. During my 'apprenticeship' at the *Evening Telegraph* (then in Dryland Street) I was one of the regular gang of reporters who enjoyed free early-evening performances at The Granada after work with the flash of a press card. We must have seen virtually every film released from 1972 until the cinema changed over to bingo in 1974. I can assure you this doesn't work at cinemas today!

Many readers, I'm sure, will remember Kemp's bicycle shop on the corner of Dryden Street and Rockingham Road, next to Reed's newsagents. John Kemp, originally from Bedford, was a marine engineer who set up the pioneering Buccleuch Cycle Works at a converted little chapel in nearby Buccleuch Street in 1886. The machines he made – built mostly with BSA fittings – won hundreds of prizes, especially at the regular Rockingham Hill climbing competitions. He opened the Rockingham Road shop in 1908, selling a range of Raleighs, Royal Enfields and New Hudsons. He also carried out repairs in the extensive workshop behind the shop, which had a separate entrance in Dryden Street. He was helped by his son, John Kemp Junior, an NCU ten-mile champion at Northampton in 1910, who took over the shop on his father's death in 1928. This picture was taken in 1959 as the premises were about to be converted into an area office and three self-contained flats by the Nottingham Oddfellows Society. The society first became established in Kettering more than a century earlier when the Shakespeare Lodge was formed. Today the premises are occupied by accountant Martin Toms.

The birth of Kettering General Hospital in 1897 was the realisation of a dream by a small band of public-spirited townspeople and businessmen. Building began in October 1895 and two foundation stones, either side of the main entrance, were laid on 9 May 1896 by Lady Brunner of Deene Park and the Duchess of Buccleuch, whose husband donated the land on which the hospital was built. By that time a public appeal, launched in 1891, had raised £5,600 towards its cost but the final fundraising event – a week-long bazaar at the Victoria Hall in Gold Street – realised an incredible £3,000. Local architects Gotch & Saunders designed the building in Rothwell Road, pictured here from the front, and of seven tenders submitted for construction work, Alfred Barlow's lowest quote of £5,575 was accepted. Kettering people turned out in force for the official opening on Saturday 30 October 1897 which followed a huge banner-waving parade through the town led by the Rifle Band and the Royal Bucks Hussars. Earl Spencer, as the county's Lord Lieutenant, had been asked to perform the opening ceremony, but withdrew at the 11th hour following the death of his friend, the Duchess of Teck. His place was taken by his brother, the Right Hon C. R. Spencer, who arrived in an open horse and carriage, seated with hospital pioneer John Turner Stockburn and architect John Alfred Gotch. The hospital was initially run by a board of governors, a mixture of leading citizens and doctors, with Mr Stockburn as president. A total of 129 patients were treated in the first year, the running costs of £1,500 met mostly by endowment funds, annual subscriptions and factory collections.

Kettering General Hospital

This rare early picture of the hospital (right), taken circa 1904, shows how the complex looked from behind. It began with two adult wards of ten beds (named Spencer and Buccleuch), with room for two children's cots in each. These were built either side of the main entrance block, which housed a third ward with two beds for private patients. All wards were linked by a central corridor, with bathrooms and lavatories in separate blocks at each end. There was an operating room, drugs store, dining room and an office for the first matron, Miss Gertrude Hick, who also had a bedroom upstairs along with sleeping quarters for five nurses. In December 1902 the Earl of Dalkeith opened an £8,000 extension, which included a new ward, new waiting and consulting rooms and a new operating theatre. Each ward, heated by two stoves, also had windows overlooking extensive grounds, seen here, which included vegetable gardens and an orchard, supplying healthy home-grown food for patients.

This ramshackle, derelict building (left) awaiting demolition in 1982 was originally known as Kettering Isolation Hospital. Situated on the east side of Rockingham Road, it provided accommodation for patients with infectious diseases and treatment for cases of measles, influenza, pneumonia, whooping cough and acute diseases of the nervous system. Erected in 1886, the original complex – known by many as the "fever hospital" – was set in several acres of grounds, with alterations in 1916 and 1928. These included extensions to the administration block, providing four bedrooms, a new kitchen and scullery. By 1935, it consisted of seven blocks – administration offices, night nurse accommodation, scarlet fever ward, cubicle block, diphtheria ward, general cases of infection ward and laundry room. Although it could accommodate up to 70 patients, only six beds were occupied that year, when the matron was Miss J. B. Stuart. In an article in the *Kettering Leader* in March 1935, the county medical officer Dr J. M. Mackintosh described the hospital as a "feather in Kettering's cap" and it was seemingly state-of-the-art. The report says the laundry "includes a Robot drier, hot air from which drives the moisture from the washing as it is gently stirred and moved about by means of automatically-operated clothes lines."

Historic Barton Seagrave Hall in Barton Road, pictured right when it was still fully visible from Polwell Lane, is a Grade II listed building with a Grade I listed orangery, once occupied by the 18th century historian John Bridges, who wrote *The History and Antiquities of Northamptonshire*. For many years until 1911, the hall – partly Elizabethan in style – was the home of Viscount Hood. In 1928 Charles Wicksteed bought it on behalf of the Wicksteed Village Trust with the idea of turning it into a hostel for people with limited means, but it became a guest house. After his death it became the Fellowship Home for the Elderly, run by a national trust based in Surrey. The Wicksteed Trust bought it back in 1954 and it continued to be an old people's home, renamed the Wicksteed Memorial House in his memory and enlarged to provide four more rooms. After closing in 2001 there were plans to turn it into a luxury hotel with the aid of lottery cash, but in June 2003 Northamptonshire Healthcare NHS Trust was hoping to lease the building as offices while it builds a new mental health unit on the site of St Mary's Hospital.
(*Tony Smith Collection*)

This photograph from 1952 was taken when a Horsemarket building known as "The Puzzle" was in the final stages of demolition. The 19th century block – to the left of the Cross Keys Restaurant (now O'Malley's pub) – posed such a danger that it was dismantled brick by brick, as seen in the picture. A picture of the building just before demolition began appeared on page 114 of my book *20th Century Kettering*, when I was unable to explain how the building got its nickname. In its lifetime it had been occupied by a variety of businesses and the upper floors were once flats. Buried in one of Fred Moore's random notebooks is his explanation for the strange soubriquet, dating from 1884. Apparently it stemmed from a then revolutionary scheme by the owner John Carrington to convert the three-storey building into tenements. The notes say: "It was too good a thing to pass unnoticed at the time, hence it was called "The Puzzle", the public being utterly puzzled to understand how Mr Carrington had fitted the narrow parts together, to say nothing of the ingenious contrivances for stowing away shutters, other peculiar methods of economising space." In conclusion, the notes add: "John Carrington was considered eccentric, some considered him a subject for the lunatic asylum, but for all that he was a clever man."

The exterior of Hawthorn Road School has changed little since this photograph (left) was taken in 1925. It was erected by the School Board in 1894 to cater for children of the fast-expanding southern end of the town, but was not officially opened until May 1895. Costing £2,800, it was designed by Gotch & Saunders and built by Kettering contractor George Valentine Henson of Victoria Street. Initially there were three infant classes with 94 pupils, under headmistress Miss Elizabeth Clark, with Miss Brookes as her assistant. By 1903 the average attendance was 115 and two years later a junior school with six classes was built on site by Mr O. P. Drever. This added around 300 to the roll call, with William Cartwright as headmaster. In the early part of the last century, pupils wrote on slates with slate pencils, discipline was strict and boys and girls were segregated in the playground. When it was first opened, the house pictured to the right of the school was occupied by Harry Rootham. Today it is a butcher's shop run by Paul Harris, who went to Hawthorn School (the "Road" has since been dropped from its name) and lives round the corner in Roundhill Road. (*Tony Smith Collection*)

Pictured right is the old Parish Church School in Horsemarket before it closed in the mid-1960s, its pupils transferring to the new Bishop Stopford School in Headlands. The building, made of red brick with stone framework for its Gothic-style windows, was originally the Boys' National School, built in 1873 on land donated by the Duke of Buccleuch. Complete with the Master's House, it was erected by Charles Sharman for around £1,500 with running costs met mainly by voluntary subscription and a weekly fee of a penny per pupil. At first it catered for up to 200 boys up to the age of 13 and when Regent Street builders Charles & Frederick Henson carried out alterations in 1905, classes transferred to the Toller Sunday Schools. When the Boys' National School ceased to exist under the education system revamp of the 1920s, its metamorphosis into a mixed senior school for over-11s was overseen by Frederick Potter, its headmaster since 1916. Its name changed to the Parish Church School in 1927, its first intake of pupils coming from the former Market Hill Girls' School and nearby Church Walk Infants, but later St Mary's, St Andrew's and Henry Gotch were the main feeder schools. The building was demolished in September 1970 and a memorial plaque was incorporated into the paving of the new garden area there three years ago. (*Tony Smith Collection*)

This sorry-looking photograph of the former St Andrew's Church of England School in St Andrew's Street was taken in June 1964 before it was demolished to make way for a car park and the new inner ring road. It had closed two years earlier and its pupils moved to its present site in Grafton Street. The first St Andrew's School in Kettering (also known as North End School) was built in Northall Street in 1859 for 200 infants. The building in St Andrew's Street was a mixed school for 385 children, erected in 1884 at a cost of £1,200. An early influence was William Barber, headmaster in the late 19th and early 20th century. In more recent history Miss Margaret Smith was headmistress for 28 years until 1959 and the school's last headmaster was the inimitable Claude Oglethorpe. My only memory of St Andrew's School was attending rehearsals for a production of the musical *Noye's Flude* (Noah's Flood) performed by pupils from several Kettering schools, including Grange Primary, which I attended. The musical director was the legendary Gladys Riseley, a fearful experience for a timid boy of six or seven, I can assure you! The site of St Andrew's School is roughly in the area of the present-day Eskdaill Medical Centre.

When it was built in 1939, Henry Gotch School in Windmill Avenue was the most modern in the county. It was officially declared open on Friday, June 30 that year by the HM Chief Inspector of Schools Mr E. G. Savage, who was a late replacement for the Education Secretary Kenneth Lindsay who was taken ill. The school had two separate blocks of buildings – the junior accommodating 384 pupils in eight classrooms, with desks for 48 children in each. The infants, sited on the south side, provided for 336 pupils in seven classrooms in addition to a 40-place nursery. The biggest of the classrooms doubled as a dining room and each school had a large assembly hall, with staffrooms overlooking the playgrounds and playing fields. The initial intake was around 300 pupils at each school under the headships of Mr D. P. Birtwhistle and Miss J. Tate. The *Kettering Leader* report on the school opening was headed: "Kettering is in vanguard of education." The picture here of six and seven-year-olds enjoying group reading outdoors was taken in July 1963 by Pictorial Press of London as an example of "a model school in a county town." The school was named after the town's education pioneer Henry Gale Gotch, who sadly died two weeks after the opening, aged 90. Mr Gotch was educated at Kettering Grammar School, later returning to chair its governors. In 1869 he became secretary to the management committee of the town's former British School, was the first chairman of Kettering's education committee from 1903 to 1906 and remained a member until 1934. He also served on the county education committee and was chairman of the county secondary schools. He also served on Kettering's Board of Guardians for 22 years (chairing the urban council which replaced it in 1906) and in 1915 was elected alderman to the county council (only retiring at the age of 87). His name was also given to the neighbouring secondary school, which opened in 1953, and its modern-day re-branding as Ise Community College in 2000 upset many parents and traditionalists. (*Tony Smith Collection*)

Also taken in July 1963, this picture shows how revolutionary Henry Gotch School was when it was built 24 years earlier. The £48,000 complex, which was five years in the planning, was set in 18 acres of grounds, one of its chief features being a £2,160 subway beneath the busy Windmill Avenue. In his speech at the school's opening, Mr Savage spoke of the rising road accident toll of young children, who could be safeguarded in two ways – by preventing them from crossing a busy road and providing them with a large open space to play. He said that following a scheme in Salford, where streets had been closed to traffic so children could play in them, the infant death rate was cut from 11 to nil in a short time. A vote of thanks to the government inspector was given by the Mayor, Alderman J. Haynes, who unveiled the commemorative plaque in Windmill Avenue (which remained until new fencing was recently erected). The subway was declared open by Councillor William Sumpter, chairman of the council's estates and buildings committee, who thanked the Ministry of Education for passing the scheme and funding half of its cost. (*Tony Smith Collection*)

This distinctive three-storey factory (left), seen here early last century, had stood on the corner of Montagu Street and Wellington Street since 1887. It was built for Henry Hanger, one of the early exporters in the local footwear trade, who created a booming business, employing 500 men and women producing 6,000 pairs of boots and shoes per week. Sadly overwork took its toll and he died of heart failure in 1896 at the early age of 40. The factory he left remained the town's biggest until William Timpson erected his 'glass palace' in Bath Road in 1921 (page 138). Although lit by electric, most machinery at the Montagu Works was driven by steam power. The firm not only supplied customers in England, Scotland and Ireland but sent regular shipments to South Africa and other parts of the world. Leather dresser Frederick Sidney Bryant occupied the building for almost half a century until 1980 when it became the Midland Furniture Showrooms. In 2002 the premises were converted to luxury flats, which earned Northampton's Darby Building Company the annual Rose Bowl award given by Kettering Civic Society for the best designed local project. (*Tony Smith Collection*)

Another three-storey factory (right) with a long history came crashing down on Sunday 16 July 1967. This building, in the 'dip' of Stamford Road on the Carey Street corner, dated from 1856 and for its first 50 years was occupied by boot and shoe makers W. & T. Farey. But it ended its days as the premises of Chapman's box manufacturers, founded by Harry Wells Chapman in Mill Road, Wellingborough in 1888. The firm, later called Chapman Packaging, was taken over by McCorquadale Print in a £6.5 million deal in 1986 and still had factories in Wellingborough and Rushden when it celebrated its centenary. The Kettering factory was demolished in only nine hours by contractors Peter Bennie. The cleared site allowed neighbouring garage H. A. Saunders to expand. It was later Mann Egerton and is now Corby Motors. (*Tony Smith Collection*)

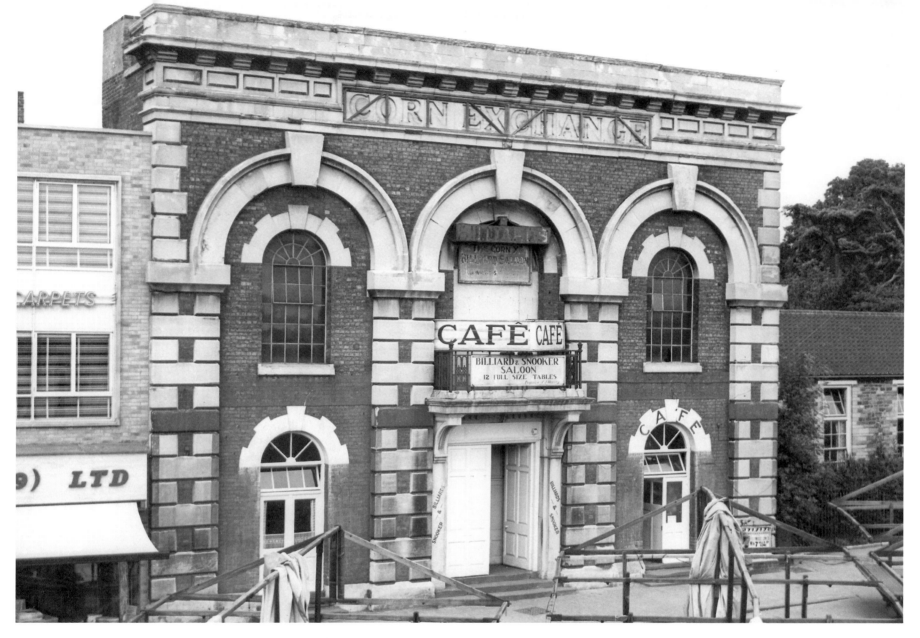

The Corn Exchange on Market Place, pictured here in July 1958, was an immense undertaking when it was built in 1853. A company was formed to purchase John Strange's old grocers shop and the total project cost £3,000, raised locally in £5 shares. It was built by joint contractors William Henson and J. Wilson to plans drawn up by Francis Edmund Law of Northampton, who also designed the old Grammar School in Gold Street (page 139). At first the market room downstairs was used for the buying and selling of corn, while the upper room became the town hall and later the town's first library. It was also hired out for concerts, dances, meetings, exhibitions and private functions. It served as a chapel when the parish church was restored and as a court when alterations were made to the Petty Sessions House. Most famously, after a corn exchange was built at the cattle market in London Road and the purpose-built library opened in 1904, it became a theatre and cinema, seating 600. Today the words COMEDY, DRAMA, TRAVEL and OPERA can still be seen on the facade, recalling the days when Harry Tate and Lillie Langtry trod the boards there. The building also bears a plaque saying the first moving pictures were shown there in 1909, when it was acquired by London cinema chain owner Leo Vint and named Vint's Electric Palace. But arguably this happened in 1903 when animated pictures of 10,000 subjects were shown there by a touring 'stereoscope' show. New owners changed its name to The Palace (1912) and The Hippodrome (1917). Down the decades the Corn Exchange has housed everything from a billiard hall to an indoor market. Today it is occupied by shops, a bookmakers, cafeteria and gymnasium.

It was the end of an era when the former Timpson shoe factory in Bath Road was demolished to make way for housing in July 1996. The imposing building was the flagship of the empire built by founder William Timpson, who began making shoes in his garden shed in Station Road in 1865. By 1884 he had progressed to a small factory in Market Street, which was later enlarged until, by 1919, 7,000 pairs were made every week. The magnificent new factory at North Park was built in 14 months but had been in production less than a year when director Thomas Mursell – the driving force behind the project – died in November 1923. For many years the building (nicknamed the 'Crystal Palace' because of its expanse of windows) was an example of what a factory should be like – the architecture, the heating and air systems, the great pains taken to keep it clean and pleasant, were all quite novel at the time. By the outbreak of the Second World War, weekly output had risen to 17,000 pairs of shoes even before the firm was contracted to provide army boots for our fighting forces. New methods of manufacture and the growing import of cheap foreign footwear since the 1950s both contributed to the firm's decline and 800 workers lost their jobs when the factory closed in 1972. (*Tony Smith Collection*)

This photo (right) taken near the bottom of Tanners Lane in the 1960s shows some of the old buildings, including the ventilating tower of the 1904 maltings, which once belonged to the Crown Brewery in Gold Street. Beer had been brewed in Kettering since the early 19th century and sold from the Crown Inn pub, first by the Rose family and then from 1871 by William Elworthy & Co of Brixworth. In the 1920s a staff of 20 produced up to 400 barrels a week for two dozen tied houses in the area (each worker entitled to three free pints of beer per day). Poppies footballers were often found jobs there, including the legendary "Ducky" Draper. The brewery and pub were run by three generations of Elworthys, who at one time also owned 15 country pubs, the George Hotel and historic Beech House. A family death led to the company being sold to Marstons of Burton-on-Trent in 1931 and beer production ceased by 1940. A depot/bottle store was kept by Marstons until 1960 when it was sold to Sainsburys, who needed the land for its new store in Gold Street, which opened in 1965. (*Tony Smith Collection*)

Many postcards featuring Kettering's temporary cenotaph were published following the end of The Great War. The top two photographs on the previous page show some of the many thousands of townspeople who turned out for the first Armistice Day ceremony, held outside the library in Sheep Street on the actual anniversary of Tuesday 11 November 1919, when council chairman Lewis Richards was among those laying wreaths. Although some shops and factories gave workers a half-day off to attend, those who couldn't observed the two minutes' silence as a mark of respect. The bottom two photographs and the one on this page were taken on Sunday 7 November the following year, when it was decided to stage future remembrance services on the nearest Sunday so everyone could attend if they so wished. Placing a wreath on the bottom right picture on page 146 was the Reverend Frederick John Burt, ex-chaplain and vicar of St Andrew's Church, who led the ceremony. This was preceded by a large procession through the town from Dalkeith Place, led by 12 police constables under the command of Inspector Brittain. Ex-servicemen and members of the town's British Legion, St John Ambulance Brigade, local bands and other organisations also took part and attended a drumhead service in the Manor House Field afterwards, where Earl Spencer, then the county's Lord Lieutenant, addressed the gathering after inspecting the servicemen. Kettering had lost more than 800 men in the First World War and thousands of people were again present when the permanent stone memorial was unveiled beside the Art Gallery in 1921.

The Library in 1906

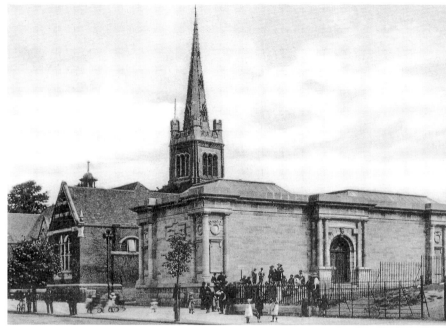

Alfred East Art Gallery in 1915

Top of Northampton Road in the 1930s

Sheep Street in the 1960s

The Alfred East Art Gallery, erected next to the library in Sheep Street, was designed by John Alfred Gotch and officially opened by Earl Spencer on 31 July 1913. Sadly Sir Alfred, widely considered the country's great living landscape artist of his era, was too ill to attend and died on 28 September that year. The work of Kettering's best-known and most accomplished painter was first recognised in 1899 when he was elected an Associate of the Royal Academy – celebrated at a special banquet in his honour at the Royal Hotel on 3 October that year. In 1906 Alfred succeeded Sir Wyke Bayliss as president of the Royal Society of British Artists, a post he held until his death. Kettering honoured him with another banquet at the Royal on 20 September 1910 to celebrate his knighthood in King George's birthday honours list of that year. When Sir Alfred presented a collection of his oils, watercolours and etching to his home town, plans were drawn up to build a gallery to put them in. When he died, his body lay in state in the gallery his gift had caused to be erected, with 7,500 townspeople queuing up to pay their personal tributes over three days. Soon afterwards a bust of Sir Alfred by Sir George Frampton was placed in the quadrangle between the art gallery and the library.

The former Kettering Grammar School and High School (Bowling Green Road)

This wonderful postcard shows a cyclist, two horse-drawn traps and cattle being driven down Bowling Green Road from the nearby cattle market in London Road in 1914. Hidden behind the huge tree in the Manor House Field is the newly-erected neo-Georgian building housing Kettering's Grammar School and High School (now, of course, the council offices), seen from different angles on the page opposite. The handsome new school was another example of the excellent designs of architect J. A. Gotch, with its imposing frontage in Bowling Green Road. When it was opened in September 1913, the building was surrounded by empty space which was never likely to be built upon to the detriment of the school. It had a central block with two projecting wings, one for boys and the other for girls. The lighting and ventilation required a large number of sash windows which, together with the widely outlying eaves and a bold cornice at the level of the top floor, gave architectural character to the building. The windows of the assembly hall, which occupied two storeys of the central block, were proportionately lofty and separated by stone columns. The tiled roof was in different shades of red and near the main hall were the kitchens, dining hall and housekeeper's room, the side wings containing classrooms and cloakrooms. Also on the ground floor were rooms for the headmaster and headmistress and for their secretaries. At the back of the middle wing were a library, science room, domestic economy room and art room. There were also medical inspection rooms, storerooms, common rooms and a manual instruction room, with a lift from the basement to the top floor. The hall (which became the council chamber when turned into municipal offices in the mid-1960s) also doubled as a gymnasium and the three main staircases were all rendered fireproof.

1910

Bottom end of Gold Street

1920s

1950s

1950s

1920s

Top end of Gold Street

1930s

1950s

1950s

153

Towards town in the 1900s

Rockingham Road

Outside St Andrew's Church in the 1950s

Cobley's grocers in 1910

Regent Street corner in 1915

1936

1906

London Road

1937

1910

1950s

1960s

Silver Street

1908

1966

Newland Street

High Street in the 1950s

Horsemarket in the 1960s

Dalkeith Place and Silver Street in the 1960s

Montagu Street in the 1950s

Windmill Avenue roundabout

Stamford Road

Kingsley Avenue

St Peter's Avenue

Eden Street

Dryden Street

Bayes Street

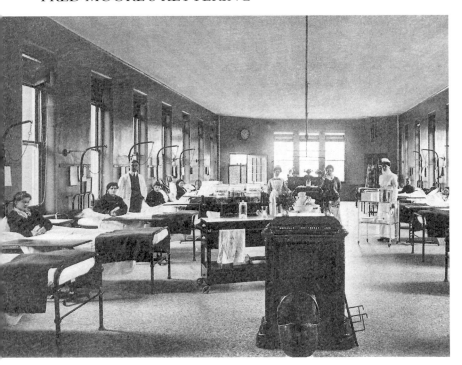
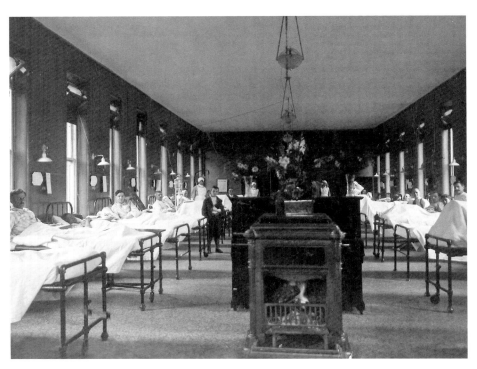

Kettering General Hospital: women's and men's wards

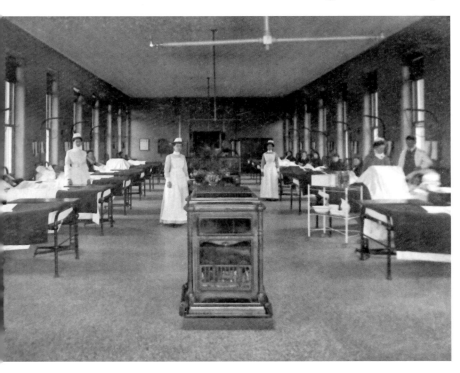
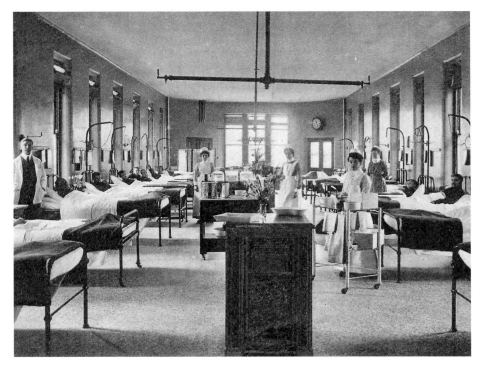

Rockingham Road Pleasure Park

Northampton Road

Top entrance

WICKSTEED PARK

Sandpit

Playground

Billy Briggs

The one and only Billy Briggs, pictured here in 1910, was a legendary Kettering carrier, who lived and died in the same house at No. 10 Rockingham Road (then facing down Northall Street but now long gone). Billy owned eight horses, stabled opposite Beech House in Tanners Lane, and his fleet of vehicles for hire included traps, dog carts, governess carts and wagonettes. His carrier's cart also took goods and parcels to Northampton every Wednesday and Saturday and on duty he would usually wear a black frock coat and tall hat. No Sunday School "Treat" was complete without a ride in Billy's wagonette (see other picture outside Hawthorn Road School), and children used to sing or recite the daft ditty: "Old Bill Briggs had six pigs and kept them down the cellar; one went ph… (raspberry noise), another went ph…, and they all went ph… together!" Many amusing yarns were told about Billy and his antics, like the one about his buying a new horse, borrowing a stool to get on its back and then getting off to see how he looked on it. It was also said that when Billy got drunk – which was quite often according to legend – his horse always knew the way home. When Billy died in July 1920, aged 85, the obituary in the *Kettering Leader* said: "He bore many of the peculiar characteristics of the driver of Victorian days. His sayings were often tinged with an unusual quaintness, although some of the stories attributed to him were not true. He prided himself on his horses in the days when factory employees went out in his brakes for their annual picnics." They sure don't make 'em like that anymore!

Charles Wise

Victorian schoolmaster and musician Charles Wise was a well-known local historian responsible for writing such important works as *The Compotus of the Manor Of Kettering AD 1292, The Montagus of Boughton, Northamptonshire Legends* and *Rockingham Castle and The Watsons*. He lived in a cosy country cottage at Weekley, where he taught at the village school and was organist at the village church. He also played tenor violin for Kettering Choral Society (always walking to rehearsals) and played works by Haydn, Mozart and Beethoven in a quartet during soirées at his home, before a light supper of bread and cheese with a glass of beer. His fellow musicians were Warkton farmer Tom Jones (accidentally killed in the harvest field), Harry Mobbs (founder of Kettering lastmakers Mobbs & Lewis) and Kettering education pioneer Henry Gale Gotch. As a schoolteacher, he was an austere bookworm and a strict disciplinarian, but was said to be polite to adults and had a kind heart. Mr Wise, whose son Stanley went to Kettering Grammar School, often gave talks on local history to Kettering Church Institute and, dressed in his Victorian hat and frock coat, never missed church, where he was also a formidable choirmaster.

Almshouses residents

These elderly ladies were residents of the historic Sawyer's Almshouses in Sheep Street, outside which they are pictured in August 1925. The Sawyers were a leading town family and Lords of the Manor for 150 years until 1723. Sea merchant Edmund Sawyer, who died in 1687, left £600 to his sister Joyce to be used to benefit the poor and these quaint houses, which survive today, were built the following year. This photograph was taken to mark the bequest of £250 to the almshouses in the will of Mrs Sophia Danner of Peterborough. Pictured standing, from left, are Mrs Pack (71), Mrs Myrenda Neal (76), Mrs Mary Shortland (76) and Mrs Anne Howard (72). Sitting in front are Mrs Spriggs (81) and Mrs Bland (82). Mrs Shortland, who died in 1932, was the first errand girl employed by Kettering Co-op and worked there for many years. She was also one of the oldest members of the town's Co-op Women's Guild and a regular at Toller Church. When the Central Hall was built, her portrait was hung in the Long Room. Mrs Neal, widow of railway worker John Neal, was born in Liverpool but came to Kettering as a young girl when her father became a horse-keeper at Pytchley. Mrs Howard, who died in 1937, was born in Rothwell but had lived in Kettering since 1871. Her late husband was local builder and carpenter Henry George Howard.

Thomas Henry Gotch

The Gotch family has been synonymous with Kettering for almost 300 years, introducing the shoe trade to the town in 1778 and the town's first bank in West Street until it unexpectedly crashed in 1857. Running the bank at that time was Thomas Henry Gotch, portrayed here that very year, who was a highly talented mathematician who produced a complex 300-page volume on logarithmic and trigonometric tables (to seven places of decimals, no less). He was also a keen amateur astronomer who used advanced maths for his calculations. After the crash Thomas Henry fled the family home of the Mission House in shame but returned to Kettering after five years' exile to revive the family fortunes, living in Newland Street until buying Chesham House from John Turner Stockburn. His four notable sons were Henry (see pages 134/5), the acclaimed artist Thomas Cooper, town architect John Alfred and shoe magnate Davis Frederick, who partnered William Timpson for eight years.

George Harrison

Kettering hairdresser turned poet-painter George Harrison died at his Bath Road home in January 1950, aged 74. On page 146 of *The Kettering Album* he is pictured with his assistant and some of his customers outside his barber shop in Gold Street in 1911. Fascinated by the countryside, he loved to sketch landscapes around his home town, which often appeared in the *Kettering Leader* and other journals with an accompanying essay or poem. He studied art in Belgium with W. B. Gash, his mentor and former art master at Kettering Grammar School. George's paintings often featured in annual exhibitions of Kettering Art Society, of which he was secretary. He was co-opted onto Kettering Education Committee in 1938 and did much to encourage an appreciation of art in local schools, to which he often donated canvasses of his work. (*Tony Smith Collection*)

Billy Eagle

Billy Eagle, of William Street, Kettering was a popular comedian and singer of comic songs who won many prizes at local talent contests and performed at local clubs, old folks' teas and numerous charity functions. His working life was in the shoe industry, first at Abbott & Bird's factory in Green Lane and then for 33 years at Frank Wright's factory in Carey Street until retiring in 1931. He began singing silly songs as a young boy to help family finances and won comic singing competitions at the coronations of both Edward VII and George V. At Christmas in 1893 he arranged and performed at the first concert party at the old workhouse in London Road, a custom he continued for more than 50 years, by which time it had become St Mary's Hospital. For some years Billy was a choirboy at the parish church, where he and wife Elizabeth were one of three couples wed simultaneously by Canon Lindsay on 4 October 1885. Elizabeth, whose father Charles Holmes was for many years platform manager at Kettering railway station, was Billy's childhood sweetheart when their parents lived in Duke Street. The couple had 8 children and 11 grandchildren, many of whom sang in church choirs. As a comic Billy had engagements from a wide area but his jokes were never vulgar or objectionable, often re-writing lyrics of songs if he thought they might cause offence to the ladies. During his long career as an entertainer, he appeared in Pierrot troupes, minstrel groups and so-called 'nigger' troupes, duetting with his friend Tom Harris – he as "Bones" and Tom as "Sambo" – but he turned down offers to tread the boards full-time. In retirement he was secretary of Kettering Pensioners' Parliament, which he helped found.

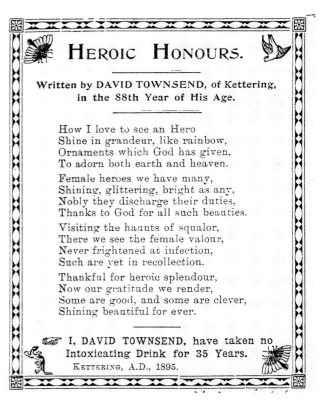

HEROIC HONOURS.

Written by DAVID TOWNSEND, of Kettering,
in the 88th Year of His Age.

How I love to see an Hero
Shine in grandeur, like rainbow,
Ornaments which God has given,
To adorn both earth and heaven.

Female heroes we have many,
Shining, glittering, bright as any,
Nobly they discharge their duties,
Thanks to God for all such beauties.

Visiting the haunts of squalor,
There we see the female valour,
Never frightened at infection,
Such are yet in recollection.

Thankful for heroic splendour,
Now our gratitude we render,
Some are good, and some are clever,
Shining beautiful for ever.

I, DAVID TOWNSEND, have taken no
Intoxicating Drink for 35 Years.
KETTERING, A.D., 1895.

David Townsend

David Townsend (1807–96) was a clever yet eccentric Calvinist and Puritan who travelled far and wide to address Temperance meetings but was equally at home as a travelling tinker and street entertainer. This bookish son of a farm bailiff at Grafton Underwood studied Latin and gave lectures on a number of serious subjects, including one to the Mutual Instruction Society at Kettering on the "Ancient Geography of Babylonia"! He was a blacksmith in Geddington before coming to Kettering in 1859, where he later signed the pledge in engineer Owen Robinson's house and became a staunch Temperance advocate. But in later life he was a familiar figure in town, wearing knee breeches, coloured waistcoat, long coat and hat. His favourite 'perch' was on a windowsill at the top of Station Road, where he would spend practically all day playing his fiddle and reciting his poems and songs, which he also sold in small booklets. The chorus of a famous song he composed for Queen Victoria's Diamond Jubilee went: "In the reign of two Georges and William I've been, and 59 years under our Royal Queen." David, who lived in Gold End, Lower Street, is pictured with his fiddle in this 1882 photograph by Alfred Knighton.

W. H. Baker

This is how Walter Henry Baker advertised his shop, pictured on page 24. Although originally from Hull, Mr Baker soon immersed himself in town life as chairman of the Chamber of Trade and member of the Board of Guardians and urban council. He was also founder chairman of Kettering's Small Holdings Association and president of Kettering Harriers, where he was a good runner and exponent of ju-jitsu and weight-lifting. He was probably best known, however, as an ingenious inventor of everyday things, a talent he discovered as a schoolboy. In 1884 he claimed to have invented the white line system for traffic control after witnessing a collision between a farm cart and carrier's van – immediately borrowing a whitewash brush and drawing a line on the roadway at the crash scene! His other creations included a special glove for traffic police, the heating of railway carriages by steam (previously done with hot water bottles) and a device known as "Baker's Nail" – similar to white line studs, which he tried out in Gold Street and Bowling Green Road. He sold the patent to a Coventry firm, which produced a modified version in great numbers. When his Kettering business closed down, Mr Baker, who had a son and two daughters, went to live in Hove, where he died in his early 60s. Returning to the main picture, the white-bearded gentleman drumming up business for Mr Baker was Sam Bright, nicknamed "Smang" (a combination of "Sam" and "Bang").

Ulrick Aeschlimann

George Jessop

Swiss-born Ulrick Aeschlimann was a highly-respected and skilled watch and clockmaker in Tanners Lane. He came to Kettering in 1872 after learning his trade in Birmingham, Leicester and Peterborough. For six years he worked for his father before carrying on a thriving business at the same shop for 44 years, acquiring much property in the town centre. He took a keen interest in local politics, writing witty letters to the local authorities and was associated with the Labour Party for many years. As a Swiss he encountered difficulties in his attempts to vote before he was naturalised. Local children, unable to pronounce his name, called him "A Silly Man". He had heart trouble in his declining years and spent the last week of his life in bed under Dr Lee's orders. The father-of-three, who lived in Stamford Road, died on 15 October 1922, leaving three sons.

Kettering builder, carpenter and undertaker George Jessop (1840–1924) was the son of William Jessop of Rothwell and born at the family's home in Workhouse Lane (now Dryland Street). He attended the nearby British Schools and when old enough worked with his father at a wood yard next to Palmer's Music Stores in Silver Street. His father died while sawing a tree trunk over a sawpit, falling into the pit and breaking his neck. In 1860 George married Ann Shatford and they lived in the old workhouse master's house (on the site later occupied by the *Evening Telegraph*), bringing up nine children. George, who had a workshop in an adjacent square, was actively involved with the Band of Hope, held many offices at the Silver Street Wesleyan Church and was a teacher and superintendent of its Sunday School for 60 years. In his 30s he campaigned with Owen Robinson against compulsory vaccination and was often fined by courts.

J. T. Stockburn

This photograph of the legendary and indefatigable John Turner Stockburn (1825–1922) was taken on his 90th birthday. You could write an entire book on the public service and achievements of this Kettering draper's son, who was rightly regarded as the 'founder' of Kettering General Hospital. This successful stay and corset-maker first raised the subject as chairman of the Local Board and presided at a public meeting in November 1891, when he offered the first £500 to the venture. He became the first chairman of the governors of the new hospital when it opened in 1897. He was also founder member and chairman of the town's Gas Company and Waterworks Company, chairman of the Northamptonshire Printing & Publishing Company (then owners of the *Kettering Leader* and *Evening Telegraph*) and one of the county's first middle-class JPs. He was an active Congregationalist, first at Toller Church and later the London Road Chapel, where he was a long-serving treasurer. Mr Stockburn held a lifelong interest in politics and local government. He was a staunch Liberal who helped form the North Northants Liberal Association in the late 1870s, becoming first vice-president and then its president. He went on to chair the newly-formed East Northants Liberal Association in 1885, helped establish the Liberal Club in Dalkeith Place in 1889, and was president of the constituency Liberal Party from 1885 to 1910, when Francis Channing was returned as MP seven times in succession. Stockburn himself stood for North Northants in 1892 but lost out to Lord Burghley by 669 votes. In local government 'J.T.S.' was elected to the first Local Board in 1872, which he chaired from 1890 to 1894, and went on to chair its successor, Kettering Urban District Council, from 1894 to 1898. He also represented the town on the first county council from 1889 to 1892. With all of this on his plate it was a wonder the great man – who also served on numerous other committees – had time to become a successful businessman and father of seven children. After leaving school, Stockburn was apprenticed to a draper in Canterbury for four years before returning to Kettering in 1844 to join the drapery his father ran with John Goosey. Partnered by his brother-in-law Robert Wallis, he later established his own corset factory in Northall Street in 1874 and after Mr Wallis died in 1857, carried on for another 30 years before passing it over to his sons. For many years Stockburn lived at the Mission House in Lower Street, where he entertained General Booth during the Salvation Army founder's visit to Kettering in 1907. After retiring, he even ran a farm and rode with the Pytchley Hunt.

Mr & Mrs Starmer

George Henry Starmer and his wife Ann, pictured (left) after their 66th wedding anniversary in 1936, claimed to be Kettering's (and possibly the county's) oldest and longest married couple. Then both 84, they were wed at the parish church on 30 October 1870 and later had two daughters and 12 sons, 19 grandchildren and nine great-grandchildren. George was born in Hazelwood Lane and Ann in Northall Street and, when they moved into the Sackville Street home where they lived for 45 years, there were no houses north of St Andrew's Church and a windmill stood in a nearby field which later became Dryden Street! Mr Starmer, a shoe hand who served in The Great War with the Volunteer Training Corps, was among the pioneers of the Blue Violet Lodge of the Manchester Unity Order of Free Gardeners, founded in 1875. In 1894 he joined the Pytchley Lodge of the Buffaloes, later served on the hospital sports committee and was a bell-ringer for many years. Mrs Starmer died five weeks after Spencer Percival took this picture.

Mr & Mrs Dix

This picture, taken outside their home in Melton Street, Kettering, shows sprightly newlyweds Mr and Mrs Samuel Dix, both aged 87. Because they were both over 80, they had to get a special licence to get married, but this was not the only reason the union made the local headlines in 1924. The ceremony took place on Monday 5 May – just eight days after the sad departure of Mr Dix's first wife Eliza. She died at an address in London Road on Sunday 27 April and was buried on Wednesday 30 April, but the *Kettering Leader* story wasn't published until 16 May. Tantalisingly, it does not identify the new Mrs Dix or give any further details and no pre-wedding announcement was made in the official notices. Under the headline "Widower For A Week," the report says: "At an age when most of us expect to be contemplating the prospect of being buried rather than married, Mr Dix has entered the matrimonial state again." Don't you just love a mystery?

Joe York

This wonderful picture of a man and his horse was taken outside Kettering's former Salvation Army headquarters in Field Street (pictured on page 102), with only the behatted rider and the rather startled boy on the far left apparently aware of the photographer! The gentleman is believed to be Joseph Skepper York of Sackville Street, who had been a member of the Kettering Corps for more than 20 years, holding the position of Envoy at the time of his death, aged 68, in September 1941. Originally from Lincolnshire, "Happy Joe" (as he was known) was for many years a popular employee of leather firm Lindrea & Company in Tanners Lane. The funeral service was conducted at Mr York's home by the Kettering commandant Major G. Coxhead, who also officiated at the subsequent burial in the London Road cemetery. This ended with the singing of 'Rock Of Ages', the favourite hymn of the deceased. Mr York left a widow Fanny, son Joe and five daughters.

Charles Wicksteed

This is the first of four pictures showing well-known people with very different forms of transport, beginning with this classic photograph of Charles Wicksteed in his two-seater Humber watching children at the boating lake of his newly-opened park in 1921. As an engineer, Mr Wicksteed was fascinated with motors and machinery, making steam ploughs, bicycles and accessories at his Stamford Road works. In 1907 he took out a motor car gearbox patent, spent much time and money enlarging the factory to make it, but almost faced ruin when he found no takers from the motor industry. It was some time before the new tools and gadgets he invented (particularly the mechanical hacksaw) made enough money to cover his losses. During the First World War the firm won lucrative government contracts for munitions and the switch to making playground equipment helped the company ride the depression of the 1920s.

Warren East

This self-portrait by Kettering bootmaker turned photographer Warren East and his horse-drawn wagon was taken beside the Eleanor Cross in Geddington. His studio was next to the Newland Street passage, later to become B. H. Miles' fish and poultry shop. Warren was a pioneer of the camera who recorded many scenes of Kettering on glass slides, many of which were rescued by Fred Moore decades later and shown on East's original "magic lantern". Some of the older pictures in this book were taken by him. Warren was also well-known as a bandmaster and cornet player for Kettering Town Band (formed in 1871) and the old Victoria Mission Band. Following his death in March 1925, several town streets were closed to traffic as an impressive parade of 90 bandsmen – from the Town, Rifle, Fuller Mission and Victoria Mission – massed to play him to the cemetery.

Reverend Frederick Cattell

Starting up this four-seater Austin 7 is the Reverend Frederick Cattell, vicar of St Andrew's Church from 1924–46 and later Canon of Peterborough. The vehicle, costing £40, was bought by his parishioners and presented to him after evensong on Sunday 27 April 1927. The money was raised, mainly in small sums, within two months after a suggestion at a church meeting by Dr William Henderson. Subscriptions were received from every street in Kettering, mostly in threepences and sixpences, but one OAP gave his 10 shilling weekly pension. After giving Holy Communion to 761 people, the busy vicar emerged from the vestry to see church council members and hundreds of people waiting. Mr J. C. Woodward, chairman of the collection committee, said it was felt a car would help him visit his congregation in all parts of the town. Mr Cattell jokingly called the car his new "assistant curate". During his ministry, various church building projects began, including the erection of a new north aisle in 1924, with the first sod cut by the vicar's wife.

Supt Curtis and Corporal Dyson

When Corporal Walter Dyson sounded the new-fangled klaxon on this new Napier Ambulance, people were said to jump from one pavement to the other. Mr Dyson, standing to the right of Superintendent Curtis, poses with the 30 hp six cylinder Rudge-Whitworth, which replaced the horse-drawn vehicle used by Kettering's St John Ambulance Brigade. It was a gift by the town's special constables, who raised £1,100 to buy it including £300 for new equipment, presented at a formal inspection in the police station yard in May 1918. The ambulance had wire wheels and a mahogany body bearing the name of "Kettering" in steel. Modern fittings included electric light, a speaking tube and medicine chest with accommodation for two stretcher cases and two sitting cases. At the handover a letter of congratulation was read out from Earl Spencer, the county's Lord Lieutenant and president of the County Red Cross and St John Committee. The previous wagon had served for 15 years!

John James Rawson

These pupils of Stamford Road School are pictured with John James Rawson, headmaster for 31 years, sitting in the easy chair they presented to him on his retirement in July 1923. Born at Selton, Nottinghamshire in 1861, Mr Rawson began his teaching career as assistant master at Kirkby Woodhouse in Staffordshire and was later appointed head of the British School at Louth, Lincolnshire. He came to Kettering in December 1891 as the first master to open the new Board School at Toller Church. When Stamford Road School opened the following year, he became its first headmaster, at one time responsible for 800 pupils during the day and a further 600 in evening classes. In his younger days he was a keen cricketer, playing for Kettering Wanderers and Lord Lilford's XI. Other interests included raising poultry and he chaired the Kettering and District Fanciers' Association for 21 years. Mr Rawson died at his London Road home after a short illness in December 1949, aged 88. His wife had died in 1910 and he left a son and two daughters – Miss E. Rawson taught at the town's Central School.

Eagle-eyed readers who bought my last book *20th Century Kettering* will have spotted a familiar face among the children pictured outside Stamford Road School in the final end-paper photograph. This similar shot, seen close-up, reveals a mysterious moustachioed man in prison uniform looking suspiciously like Charlie Chaplin! Debate still rages over whether this was the silent movie legend himself or merely a lookalike, hired to publicise one of the star's films being shown at The Pavilion during the 1920s. A series of conflicting reports and readers' letters appeared in the *Evening Telegraph* during the 1970s, one of them even suggesting that Chaplin stayed for two weeks at a house in Wadcroft (owned by Susannah Hawthorne) while the star made a number of personal appearances. Local children were said to have waited for hours outside the house for a glimpse of their hero who led them around the town, dressed in a convict's uniform with shoes on the wrong feet. There were even varying claims about the exact film being publicised. Was it *The Circus* (1928) for which Chaplin won an Academy Award playing a man on the run from police joining a circus? Was it *The Prisoner* or *The Escaped Convict*, of which no records exist but may have been early films made before Chaplin became famous? Or was it the 1923 film *The Pilgrim*, in which he played an escaped criminal mistaken for a clergyman? Fred Moore always insisted it was the latter and that the Kettering 'Chaplin' was a fake. Who am I to differ?

William Hircock

William Timpson

William Hircock, who died in 1909, aged 95, was a well-known Kettering farmer, whose family were timber merchants in Laxton. For 70 years he lived at an old farmhouse in Montagu Street (pictured on page 51 of *The Kettering Album*). First he worked as a gardener for the Reverend Henry Corrie when he was rector and planted the avenue of trees from the parish church to Sheep Street. Then he worked for the Duke of Buccleuch, farming land on which much of the Stamford Road estate was built. Later he owned 80 acres of ploughing fields where Eden Street and Eskdaill Street now stand. When Queen Victoria passed through Kettering in 1844, William was one of the Yeomen who guarded her coach from Northampton to Weldon. He married the rector's housekeeper and they had two daughters and four sons. Shortly before he died, he enjoyed his first ride in a motor car with cycle shop owner Harry Taylor and was even induced to take the wheel for a short distance!

The life of legendary shoemaker William Timpson (1849–1929) was a classic rags-to-riches story. This son of a poor Rothwell silk weaver was making leather shoe laces at the age of eight and four years later was working in the Manchester shoe shop run by his brother Charles. At 16 he opened his first shop in the city with brother-in-law Walter Joyce, but struck out on his own, making £1,000 profit in his first year. His brilliant business brain built up an empire of retail and repair shops all over England, stocked by quality shoes made at the factory he opened in Market Street, Kettering in 1884. For almost 40 years he held a first-class rail season ticket from Kettering to Manchester as he flitted between the two each week. By the turn of the last century his son, also William, helped control the still-booming business, but illness forced the elder William to take a back seat in later years. Sadly it also meant he never set foot in the magnificent new North Park factory, which became the crowning glory of the Timpson empire from the 1920s.

Kettering's Special Constables 1914–1918

With so many young men serving in The Great War – many never to return – it became the responsibility of their fathers and others of their generation to assist with policing duties in Kettering. In recognition of the work done by the Voluntary Police Force, as they were then known, the entire unit of special constables was entertained to a dinner organised by the urban council, at which each man received an artistically-designed testimonial bearing the words: Northamptonshire Constabulary, Kettering Division, European War 1914–1918. This photograph, taken in June 1919, shows members of No. 2 Company. They are (all left to right): Back row: H. E. Munn, R. L. Knight, H. W. Bird, A. H. Abbott, E. W. Felce, A. G. Wilson, A. E. Munn. Second row: J. H. Marlow, W. S. Townley, R. N. Tarry, F. Monk, J. Norris, F. A. Potter, J. C. Brown, H. Robinson, A. Cheney, C. J. Olive, B. Ward, E. Thompson, H. W. Davis, C. Riddey. Third row: A. Bailey, T. E. Sharpe, H. W. Wallis, Geo. Wright, W. W. Lunn (leader), W. G. Burnham (leader), E. Rice, F. Shatford, J. Bond, S. T. Patrick. Front row: H. G. Roughton, T. G. Wright, S. T. Morris, T. Coles, Ernest Woodcock, A. Mee.

Sorry, folks, but I just couldn't resist the temptation to use these strangely similar, yet dissimilar photographs, if you see what I mean. This chap with the curious 'listening' stick is pictured at work on the forecourt of the Central Garage in Dalkeith Place (out of picture on the left) in 1924. The instrument, being used by waterworks inspector George Rowe, was known as a stethoscope. Although it had no medical use, it enabled the user to locate leakages of water from the Kettering main.

This distinguished gentleman – the Archdeacon of Oakham, no less – is not stooping to pick up a coin, but putting one down to begin a 'mile of pennies' along Rockingham Road in 1927. The event was arranged by members of All Saints Church to boost its Million Penny Fund to replace the iron chapel in William Street with a proper building. Coins were placed on a white line which ran from Havelock Street to Kingsley Avenue and in Pollard Street and William Street. The Archdeacon was a friend of the vicar, the Reverend G. R. J. Round, and the Diocese had promised £1,000 towards the fund. Women helpers in fancy dress raised more money by playing a barrel organ at various vantage points in the town.

Watercress Harry

This picture of one of the town's best-known characters is different to that featured on page 150 of my book *The Kettering Album* and it allows me to add further details which I have unearthed since then. Watercress Harry, after whom the Market Street pub is named, was a popular hobo who sold watercress and cabbages for beer money. Originally from Wharf Street, Leicester, the former prize fighter once worked as a master ladies' shoe hand and was always complaining about his feet. He took to the open road after a row with his girlfriend and came to Kettering, where he slept in barns and allotment huts, sometimes seeking refuge in the workhouse. Often he would chase children who made fun of him, but he would never harm them. Harry acquired his watercress from the Ise Brook and his bottles of beer from the Robin Hood pub in Northall Street. After closing time he could often be found sleeping on the steps of the Salvation Army barracks in nearby Field Street. One evening the police found him drunk on the pavement outside the Rising Sun, with the bung from a beer barrel, painted red, stuck on the end of his nose. He once fell victim of a wager by the Preston family, who were managers at Kettering Furnaces and lived at what is now SATRA House in Rockingham Road. For a bit of fun they gave him a bath and dressed him up in a fancy suit with a silk top hat. They then told him to go to the Newland Street studio of photographer Warren East, who would take his photograph and give him half-a-crown. Unfortunately that picture does not appear in Fred Moore's collection! Letters to the *Evening Telegraph* claiming Harry eventually married and settled in Thrapston were completely untrue. He died in the workhouse in 1912 and was apparently "succeeded" by a Mr Mabbutt who sold watercress and smoked haddock in Kettering, a fact I have been unable to confirm.

Kettering Salvationists assembled in force on Friday 3 August 1928 to pay their last respects to their beloved colleague George Vivian Ibbett, who died two days before his 32nd birthday after an attack of pleurisy. Mr Ibbett, whose father was a fruiterer in Montagu Street, was a prominent member of the Kettering Corps, joining as an officer in 1921, having been demobbed from the army in 1919. He had commanded a number of districts, including Leicestershire and Bushill Park, London. Pictured here is the horse-drawn funeral cortege in Bowling Green Road en route to the London Road cemetery. The funeral was attended by the town's Salvation Army Band, under deputy bandmaster Mr J. Whitmore, and Brigadier Pimm from the Army headquarters in Canterbury. A memorial service was also held at the corps' hall in Field Street on Sunday 5 August. Mr Ibbett left a wife Ethel, the daughter of a late officer, whom he married in 1922. (*Tony Smith Collection*)

This procession, (right) passing the library and Manor House Field in April 1909, was in honour of Councillor Samuel William Taylor, who died aged 54 after a long illness. The cortege included his fellow Kettering councillors led by chairman Mr J. E. Reesby, vice-chairman Henry Barlow and town clerk John Bond. Mr Taylor was a builder and foreman to Mr W. J. Payne for almost 30 years and a councillor for 14 years. He was born in Desborough, moved to Great Easton when he married and came to Kettering in 1894, living first in Mill Road and then Carlton Street. He was on the education committee and chaired the water committee and the streets and buildings committee. He was vice-chairman of the council in 1904 and became a friend of Andrew Carnegie, benefactor to the library which opened that year. Mr Ibbett was also a member of Kettering Trades Council since its formation 21 years earlier.

It's amazing what you stumble across when researching a local history book. This old picture of a beauty contest line-up was among family photographs I found following the death of my mother Joan (nee Hart) in 1986. Although spotting my mum in the middle (No. 8), nothing was written on the back and I forgot all about it until accidentally finding the same picture (and the full story behind it) in the *Kettering Leader* in 1945. The contest took place during a dance at the Central Hall on Thursday 13 September as part of a fundraising drive to buy little comforts for Merchant Navy seamen away at war (including my father Rodger Smith). Merchant Navy Week, with a set target of £2000, was launched at a dance at Wicksteed Park on Saturday, 22 September, when the winner of Thursday's beauty contest would be crowned and go on to attend other fundraising events the following week. Alas my mum was neither the winner nor among the runners-up (I demand a re-count!). The lucky lady was attractive, dark-haired Miss Eileen Mary Coe, daughter of Mr and Mrs Walter Coe, of Duke Street, Kettering. "I don't know what to say," she said, "I never dreamed of being chosen from the 13 finalists." The judges were Mayoress Mrs K. E. Tew and newly-elected Kettering MP Gilbert Mitchison, who took four factors into consideration – carriage, features, figure and general appearance. The Mayoress presented the 'Queen' with a sheaf of chrysanthemums. After the official crowning at Wicksteed Park, Miss Roe was introduced to the audience at the Regal Cinema by its manager Jack Goldy. Also present were the Queen's four attendants – Mrs Megan Brown of Cransley Road, Broughton, Miss Marie Bosworth of Stamford Road, Kettering, Miss Pauline Norman of Kettering Road, Broughton and Mrs Gwen Patrick of Cransley Road, Broughton. The pictured finalists (from left to right) are: Miss Coe, Mrs Brown, Miss Kathleen Spence of Kettering, Miss Marie Taylor of Kettering, Miss Joan Shatford of Kettering, Miss Bosworth, Mrs Joan Smith of Kettering, Mrs Patrick, Miss Sheila Walker of Kettering, Miss Pauline Norman of Broughton, Miss Dorothy Mills of Cransley, Miss Kathleen Heads of Kettering and Miss Jean Sallabanks of Kettering. At the back between contestants 12 and 10 is Mr Summerley, chairman of the hospital board, and far right is Mr S. Knibb, secretary of the local British Legion. (*Tony Smith Collection*)

In October 1914 Kettering people were asked to give temporary homes to refugees from Belgium and Northern France, whose homes were destroyed in the war. This task was co-ordinated by the local War Distress Committee whose secretary, town clerk John Bond, issued a public plea in a letter to the *Kettering Leader*. Very few refugees, mostly peasants, tradesmen and their families, could speak English and were taken in by residents for at least six months. Pictured are some of the first batch of 34 – nine men, six women and nineteen children. Because of the language barrier, two empty three-storey houses in School Lane, bought to extend the Wallis & Linnell factory, were loaned free by the clothing company and furnished by local residents and shopkeepers. Among the volunteer helpers were Mrs Roughton and Mrs Payne, joint secretaries of the Red Cross committee. Hundreds of Kettering people assembled in Station Road to greet them off the train. They carried small bundles of possessions and labels, and some of the women wept with joy. The majority had tramped via Bruges and Ghent to board the ship at Ostend and the men were found jobs by Kettering tradesmen. (*Tony Smith Collection*)

This historic picture (right) from July 1922 shows the legendary Chief Scout, General Sir Robert Baden-Powell addressing local scouts and guides on the lower lawn of "Bryn Hafod", the Hall Lane home of Charles Wicksteed, president of the district's Scouts' Association. The celebrated hero of Mafeking had arrived at Kettering station at 6.12pm to be welcomed by scouts, guides, cubs and brownies from Kettering, Loddington, Irthlingborough, Burton Latimer and Wellingborough. After inspecting the troops at "Bryn Hafod", Sir Robert addressed a public meeting at the Corn Market Hall, where he was formally welcomed by urban council chairman Ernest Woodcock. Other VIP guests included architect Mr J. A. Gotch, Kettering Grammar School head Mr J. I. Scott, and the respective vicars of St Andrew's and St Mary's Churches, the Reverend F. J. Burt and the Reverend F. H. Glaister. Pictured on either side of Mr Wicksteed are his daughter Hilda, district commissioner of the Guides' Association, and Captain H. Butlin, district commissioner of the Scouts' Association. On either side of "Big Wolf" (as Baden-Powell was known) are the Reverend H. W. Shakel, county commissioner of the Scouts' Association, and district scout master Mr Baxter.

This unique photograph was taken when Kettering General Hospital celebrated its Golden Jubilee in 1947, just a year before the National Health Service was formed. Taking centre stage at the front is Miss Agnes Jackson, matron from 1935 to 1958, who helped lay the foundations of patient care before and after the introduction of the NHS. In 1960 a ward was named after this much-loved stalwart, who headed the hospital's training school for 23 years. This later became the main children's ward, but was re-named Dolphin Ward in 2002 after a £700,000 revamp. Also present on the photograph are some well-known GPs, including Dr William Ogle, my own family's doctor in my childhood. Others pictured are Dr Harold Cooper Pretty, who was in practice for a record 47 years; Dr Frank Radcliffe, who pioneered accident and orthopaedic surgery in the 1950s; Dr William Drake-Lee, senior hospital medical officer from 1948 to 1961: and Dr John Notley, after whom a day centre at St Mary's Hospital was named. Pictured here from left to right are:

front row: Matron Fox, Dr Pretty, Agnes Jackson, Dr Gibbons, Sister Maltby
second row: Sister Moralie, Dr Notley, Sister Hooper, Dr Radcliffe, Sister McEvily, Dr Pigott, Matron Hobbs, Sister Cobb
third row: Sister Bland, Dr Drake-Lee, Sister Davies, Sister Davies, Sister Wardell, Sister Saunders
back row: Dr Mandler, Sister Sherman, Dr Ogle, Dr Lock, Dr Schemilt, Mr Jackson (hospital secretary)

Tony Ireson

Nobody personified the spirit of 'Old Kettering' more than the late local historian, journalist, author and heritage campaigner Tony Ireson. When he died in February 2002, aged 88, the town lost one of its most cherished sons. Honest, modest, generous, loyal, compassionate and inspirational are just a few words that come to mind to describe my good friend and mentor, who kindly wrote the foreword to my first book, reviewed my second in the *Evening Telegraph* and to whom my last book was dedicated in 1999. Amazingly, despite his lack of mobility and fast failing eyesight, he was writing his eighth book on old Kettering when he was taken from his home town. Long overdue recognition of his tireless endeavours came in the summer of 2001 when he was the subject of glowing articles in the *Daily Mail*, *County Life* and *Saga Magazine*, although, typically, he could not understand all the fuss when TV camera crews besieged his beloved Beech Cottage (pictured above left) to tell the story of his campaign to save his home from the bulldozers in the 1970s. Thankfully he ensured the cottage's future by leaving it in the hands of the neighbouring Martha Wallis Court old people's complex. Astonishingly, he also left more than £1m in his will, most of which was bequeathed to some of the many charities and causes he had secretly supported in life. (*Tony Smith Collection*)

Fred Moore

It is only right that this book should end where it began – as a tribute to the man without whom this publication would not have been possible. Fred Moore devoted his life to preserving these precious and priceless pictures of the past for posterity and I feel pleased and proud to have played a part in presenting this marvellous collection of truly historic material for your enjoyment and, hopefully, for that of future generations. This *Evening Telegraph* picture from the 1980s shows Fred at the wheel of Kettering's famous Robinson car with borough council promotions girl Edwina Price. This 1907 12-horsepower, four-cylinder vehicle, now in the Manor House Museum, was one of three designed and manufactured by Charles Robinson, grandson of the Victorian engineer and inventor Owen Robinson. It was assembled at his Montagu Street garage, where it is pictured below with Robinson himself at the wheel in November 1948. When the car came up for sale in the 1980s, Kettering Civic Society campaigned to keep it in the town and Fred held several magic lantern shows to raise money towards its purchase. It was eventually bought with the help of a grant from the South Kensington Science Museum.

Picture index